*Theoretical Methods*
*in Social History*

This is a volume in

STUDIES IN SOCIAL DISCONTINUITY

A complete list of titles in this series appears at the end of this volume.

# Theoretical Methods in Social History

ARTHUR L. STINCHCOMBE

National Opinion Research Center
University of Chicago
Chicago, Illinois

ACADEMIC PRESS   New York   San Francisco   London
*A Subsidiary of Harcourt Brace Jovanovich, Publishers*

Sources for quotations cited herein:

*Work and Authority in Industry,* by Reinhard Bendix. New York: John Wiley and Sons, Inc., 1956. Reprinted by permission of the author.

*The Old Regime and the French Revolution,* by Alexis de Tocqueville. Translated by Stuart Gilbert. Copyright © 1955 by Doubleday & Company, Inc. Reprinted by permission of the publisher. British Empire permission from William Collins Sons & Co., Ltd., London, England.

*Social Change in the Industrial Revolution,* by Neil J. Smelser. Copyright © 1959 by the University of Chicago. Reprinted by permission of the publisher.

*The Political Sciences: General Principles of Selection in Social Science and History,* by Hugh Stretton, © 1969 by Hugh Stretton, Basic Books, Inc., Publishers, New York. Reprinted by permission.

*History of the Russian Revolution,* by Leon Trotsky. Translated by Max Eastman. New York: Simon and Schuster, Inc., 1932. Rights controlled by Estaben Volkov.

ACADEMIC PRESS, INC.
111 Fifth Avenue, New York, New York 10003

*United Kingdom Edition published by*
ACADEMIC PRESS, INC. (LONDON) LTD.
24/28 Oval Road, London NW1 7DX

Library of Congress Cataloging in Publication Data

Stinchcombe, Arthur L.
    Theoretical methods in social history.

    (Studies in social discontinuity series)
    Bibliography: p.
    1. Sociology. 2. Social history--Methodology.
I. Title. II. Series: Studies in social
discontinuity.
HM24.S762    301'.01    78-5087
ISBN 0-12-672250-1

*This book is dedicated
to my daughter, Amy,
because she has never had
a book dedicated to her.*

# Contents

PREFACE                                                                      ix

## 1  What Theory in History Should Be and Do                                 1

Why General Ideas Are Justified                                               2
The Logical Positivist Version of Research                                    3
Quantitative Methods and Theoretical Methods                                  4
Epochal Interpretations                                                       7
The Theoretical Character of Narrative                                       13
The Intellectual Tradition and This Book                                     17
Logic, Classes, and Causal Statements                                        17
A Case of Analogy                                                            19
Explication                                                                  21
History in Modern Sociology                                                  23
Empiricism and Theoretical Strategies                                        23
Technical Appendix: The Logic of Analogy                                     25

## 2  Analogy and Generality in Trotsky and de Tocqueville                    31

The Sociological Bias of Trotsky and de Tocqueville                          31
The Sociology of Authority                                                   33

Authority and Effectiveness                                                    34
The Social Construction of Authoritative Purposes                              37
Democracy, Liberty, and Authority                                             41
Authority and Inequality or "Justice"                                         42
Structures of Authority and Strategic Groups                                  46
Authority and Symbols                                                          48
Authority and Dual Power                                                       49
The Implications of the Preceding Discussion                                  50
Geographical, Social, or Political Distribution as an Index of a Process      51
The Predispositions of Systems                                               56
Principles of Cumulative Causation                                           61
Virtual Choice                                                                70
Conclusions                                                                   75

## 3 Functional Analysis of Class Relations in Smelser and Bendix    77

Smelser's Argument                                                            77
Functional Explanation of Change                                              81
"Disturbance"                                                                 83
The Problems of Running a Family                                              87
Ideal Sequence Comparison                                                     89
Comparative Histories of Roles                                                97
The Argument from Functional Completeness                                     99
The Theory and the Strategy                                                  102
Bendix on Management Ideology                                                104
Identification of Ideological Problems                                       106
The Variety of Ideological Products                                          110
Analogy between Intellectual Productions                                     111

## 4 Conclusion    115

What Makes Human Actions Analogous?                                          117
The Logic of Concepts                                                        121

REFERENCES                                                                   125
INDEX                                                                        127

# Preface

"Only things without a history are definable." The philosophical tradition summarized in Nietzsche's aphorism holds that any entity produced by a unique course of events through time cannot be adequately described by general concepts. History then is informative to the degree that things are not instances of general categories, but are instead the product of causally connected series of events that produce unique configurations in each thing. This book argues that the philosophical position of Nietzsche's aphorism is an illusion, but an illusion that reflects the difficulties of forming general concepts in history. This argument holds that general concepts in history are intellectual achievements which are more likely to be brought about by thinkers who take the problem posed by Nietzsche seriously.

Most of this book was written while I was a fellow at the Netherlands Institute for Advanced Study (NIAS). The generosity of the Dutch government makes possible a cosmopolitan intellectual environment, ideal for that kind of research that requires reflection and reading. The ratio of money for reflection to money for busily collecting data has put a dis-

proportionate value on facts rather than thought, and the forward looking policy of NIAS helps redress the balance. A seminar of the Research
Scholars' Group of the Berkeley Institute of International Studies,
especially some penetrating questions of Leo Lowenthal, pointed out a
number of weaknesses in the argument. I have tried to patch them up
as best I can. Other questions and comments also convinced me that
there are serious questions about the historical accuracy of some of the
monographs I use here to illustrate my argument. I am forced to take the
irresponsible position that historical accuracy is not my main business
here. Each reader and critic who knows the history better than I do will
have to judge how far factual inaccuracies damage my epistemological
point. Jon Elster convinced me that a chapter on David Granick and
Ronald Dore was sufficiently uncertain in its intellectual purpose that it
had better be omitted. Charles Tilly caused there to be an introduction
and a conclusion, two small matters I had neglected in the first draft.

My wife put up with living in a suburb so that I could have my year at
NIAS. When such a conflict of interest occurs in a marriage, it is illegitimate for one of the partners to appeal over the head of the other to a
general public, to argue that it was all worth it. I consequently do not
make that appeal in this preface.

# 1

# *What Theory in History Should Be and Do*

People will expect a book with a title like this one to deal with various sociological theories that have been applied to history, such as Marxism and functionalism and evolutionism and whatnot. Especially since Trotsky and Smelser appear in the same book, and one purports to be following one general theory and the other an opposed general theory, it seems irresponsible not to address the theoretical differences between them. I do not do so, and in fact I think it a useless task. The first part of this introduction is directed to explaining why I think the intellectual tasks the reader would naturally expect to be addressed in a book with this title are not addressed, and ought not be addressed by anyone. The second part of the introduction tries to explain the problem the book is addressed to.

If Whitehead's famous dictum is to be believed, then half the problem of this book will be solved in the introduction, where I explain what the question is. For I would have written neither this book nor any other book on the subject of historical methods, unless I thought that the question of how to apply social theory to historical materials, as it is usually posed, is ridiculous. One does not apply theory to history; rather one uses history to develop theory.

My main purpose in this book is to improve the question, though I argue for my version of the question by trying to suggest what the answer looks like. To state a particular application of my general position in stark form, I contend that the difference between Trotsky's Marxism, Smelser's functionalism, and de Tocqueville's conservative despair makes hardly any difference to any important question of sociological theory.

Another way to say the same thing is to assert that all the "compare and contrast" theory questions on preliminary sociological examinations that take Marx and Parsons (or Marx and Weber, or Weber and Parsons) as the axis of comparison are foolish. When it comes down to analysis of specific cases, I would urge that when they do a good job of historical interpretation, Marx and Weber and Parsons and Trotsky and Smelser all operate the same way. The purpose of this book is to find out what that same way is, and deliberately to ignore all the grandiosity of each one's larger world view to get down to historical methods, methods of thinking about historical facts.

Obviously such a precious position, that all those things we have worried about so hard and been examined on do not matter, needs to be defended. The book as a whole is a defense of that position. But let me sketch out the nature of the answer I would give, in explicit contrast to a straw man that I will construct of "the average reader's reaction to the title."

## WHY GENERAL IDEAS ARE JUSTIFIED

The first wrong thing we have been taught about theory is similar to a primary mistake in architecture about the nature of a building. We have been taught that what justifies a particular general idea is its place in a larger structure of thought, just as a room in traditional architectural thought was a convenient way to fill out the beautiful shell of a building. But a room is a place to live in, and a general idea is a device to interpret (or to guess at, or "hypothesize") facts. It is because people can live in them that buildings are a different art form from sculpture, and it is because general ideas interpret facts that a social scientist or historian should be interested in them.

When someone makes an unexceptionable statement like the foregoing in a contentious tone, it means that he or she intends to attack the usual consequences drawn from the statement. When I explain presently exactly why Trotsky thought the Petersburg proletariat was crucial to the Russian Revolution, the Moscow proletariat somewhat less important, the proletarians in the Baltic Sea fleet really crucial, I will not be denying that because Trotsky was a Marxist he was more likely to notice proletarian importance. And if the reader wants to go to all the trouble of believing the labor theory of value in order to notice those facts, I have no real objection. Likewise, when I note that Smelser observed that cotton workers whose children were outside the factory worried more about governing them, and that his noticing came partly from his functionalism, I am stating a fact of intellectual history that Smelser himself asserts.

I urge that this has nothing to do with whether a sensible social scientist can believe both things about the proletariat, that in time of revolution they can destroy Tsarism and that in 1820 in England they can worry about who is watching the kids. I further urge that if one really wants to understand the proletariat, one would be ill advised to be voluntarily ignorant of Smelser's facts in order to be a Marxist or of Trotsky's facts in order to be a professional sociologist.

The central argument of the book then is that when they are good Smelser, Trotsky, and de Tocqueville all do the same thing, and that all else, however important on preliminary examinations, is dross.

## THE LOGICAL POSITIVIST VERSION OF RESEARCH

This book is also directed against the fashion of discussing the relation of theory to facts, sired by Kant, foaled by the Vienna School, and raced past us in our statistics textbooks. This is the notion that our theory comes from some mysterious "synthetic reason," that analytic reason (mathematics, statistics, and logic) derives the facts from synthetic reason, that we then reject theories if the facts derived from them are not true, and so eliminate wrong ideas from synthetic reason. This complicated process then leaves the purified synthetic reason as science. In the extreme positivist image, theory comes from inspiration, from architectonic schemes of the sorry scheme of things entire, to be laboriously knocked down by uninspired empirical workers. It is Einstein who is supposed to be inspired, not Michelson-Morley.

The central model of positivism is that researchers are forbidden to think between the time they "posit the hypothesis" and the time they "accept or reject the hypothesis," after calculating a bit and transforming something they want to know into something they do not want to know (the null hypothesis). A really pure priest of positivism will only accept or reject the null hypothesis, never leaving the sacred precincts to make any bet about what the world is like. The extreme of positivism is only to agree to talk about which theories have been rejected by the facts.

Clearly Trotsky would not have become a leading radical statesman, nor de Tocqueville a leading conservative statesman, if they had bet only on null hypotheses. But this specious argument aside, the whole Kantian idea contradicts our everyday experience of research. We do not form a historical interpretation before finding out what was going on. Only respect for philosophical appearances could generate such an outlandish picture of a science.

The central model of the scientific process in this book is as follows. People start their research with various general notions: Trotsky that the contradictions of capitalism piled on top of those of feudalism will produce seeds of societal destruction, to be furthered by the Russion proletariat; Smelser that English workers were probably worrying about how to take care of their kids now that the kids no longer worked at home but in a factory. The question of which set of predisposing general ideas will more often put us on the right track will *not* occupy us here. It is an important question, and it may be decided someday.

The next stage is noticing a long series of facts that seem to be connected, as cause or effect, to this vague general notion. Then this collection of loosely connected facts *is arranged into a theory* of the phenomena under study. The main argument of this book is that when a theory of historical materials is good, it is *not* because in the intellectual biography of Trotsky or Smelser it was generated by Marxism or functionalism. Further, the fact are not valuable because they refute or confirm Marxism or functionalism. *Both* the generating ideas *and* those facts first examined are useful because they generate *historically specific general ideas*. The value of the rooms is that the historical facts fit in them, not that they have been derived from a general scheme for the building.

## QUANTITATIVE METHODS AND THEORETICAL METHODS

This positivist notion that a kind of thoughtless abstract empiricism is somehow being scientifically rigorous has muddied the debate about quantitative history. Most of this book has nothing to do with numbers, although I am generally an enthusiastic quantifier. I have in fact deliberately avoided some quantitative history that I admire very much, such as Simon Kuznetz's work on American national accounts. The reason is not that Kuznetz thought of this work as being separate from the task of building a macroeconomic theory to fit the facts, nor separate from the problem of guessing what people were up to when they switched from horse to canal transportation. It is rather that the fashion in quantitative history has come to be that one must agree to be voluntarily ignorant of any evidence other than numbers.

Now it turns out that numbers available for the analysis of historical questions do not provide very subtle data about what people were up to. This means that agreeing to be voluntarily ignorant of all but the numbers is much more of an intellectual sacrifice for a historian than for a modern sociologist or econometrician.

So my argument is that lots of facts, not only rigorous, numerical, "hypothesis-testing" facts, are good hard stones for honing ideas. Further, our great sociological theorists among historical workers did not in fact agree to stop thinking while looking over the facts. De Tocqueville's theory of revolution is almost completely unanticipated in conservative thought, Trotsky's theory of the Russian Revolution almost completely unanticipated in Marxist thought; they are very similar, and both are probably basically true. Derivation of facts from theory would have been worse for de Tocqueville than for Trotsky, because Marx at least (unlike, say, Montesquieu) was in the right general region where the facts of revolution lie.

But the *theory*, let alone the facts, of neither Trotsky nor de Tocqueville can be derived from their respective traditions. Both Trotsky and de Tocqueville were geniuses, and this agrees with the positivist notion that synthetic reason comes from inspiration. But both *thought about the facts*. For that intellectual operation, the Vienna School has no place, nor does "theoretical Marxism."

As the argument develops, it will become clear why I am unenthusiastic about most quantitative history. Let me state the argument in capsule form. For a number, say a count, to be theoretically interesting, it has to be a count of comparable instances. What makes instances comparable for a scientist is that those instances have an identical causal impact. Thus a count is more illuminating, the more theory and the more detailed examination of the facts went into making the instances counted comparable. But this ordinarily means that making a count should be the last stage of a scientific enterprise, a stage reached only after an extensive development of theory on what makes instances comparable. Is a proletarian in the Vyborg district of Petersburg or in the Baltic Sea Fleet equivalent in impact on the Russian Revolution to a proletarian in Moscow? Trotsky convinces me he was not (and if the proletarian was a she, in either place, she was not equivalent to a male proletarian either). Consequently, a count of proletarians in Russia in 1917 is a fact of relatively little interest.

Likewise if Smelser is right, the count of factory workers is not very illuminating in predicting working-class agitation. Instead, what we want is a count of male workers in factories who could not adequately supervise their children, because the children were no longer working in the factories under their supervision. Here again, if the factory worker was a woman, this fact had a different impact on the agitation.

The problem of quantitative history is not, then, that numbers cannot be illuminating. The problem is instead that if a scholar is going to select only one aspect of an instance (say of a proletarian) to make him comparable to the next proletarian, in preparation for counting, that scholar better have hold of the causally relevant aspect of the instances before counting.

But the usual source of numbers for historical reasoning is a process of generating counts that classifies instances by an impoverished theory. The argument of this book is that the theory involved in generating counts should be derived from a detailed construction of analogies between instances. It is because counts are too theoretical (and that often bad theory) that they denature historical inquiry before it starts. And the reason counts are bad theory, the reason they ordinarily classify together instances whose causal roles are not comparable, is *that they are not empirical enough*, that is, not oriented enough to the relevant facts creating analogies between cases.

Since I believe the legacy of regarding numbers as facts is the central positivist mistake, and is so deeply embedded in our everyday philosophy of science that the argument of the preceding paragraph will almost certainly be misunderstood, let me talk around it for awhile. Suppose I publish a number (as I have: Stinchcombe, 1974) showing how many hours people of the same salary grade in steel plants spend thinking, to show that the larger the number of subordinates a man has, the less time he spends thinking, controlling for rank (the higher the rank, the more time spent thinking). What is actually involved in constituting that number? First, classifying together an hour spent drawing a design for a machine, an hour calculating man loadings for a given product mix in a tube plant, an hour drafting a memorandum on delay times, an hour estimating the reliable life of parts in a machine so as to work out a parts inventory policy, and so on. These are all classified as "intellectual activity" or "thinking"—but an industrial administrator who confused these activities with one another would be fired within a month.

The reason I want to classify them together is that I believe that in certain respects they all have the same causes (e.g., that having a subordinate knocking on one's door will interfere with all of them) and the same effects (e.g., that successfully introducing a technical innovation will require more of such activities than will supervising an unchanging production line). The more I know about each of these "hours": (*a*) the more likely is my category, "thinking," to include exactly those things that are interfered with by subordinates; and (*b*) the more likely is it that the category will include exactly those activities disproportionately needed in innovations. The more I have successfully got the right activities, the more illuminating the counts of hours will be.

But this means first that the count itself is a theoretical creation. When I explain how the theory entered into the count, a good positivist tends to get nervous about how I am probably cheating—shaping the facts to fit the theory. When I describe all the detailed empirical analysis of instances that went into my concept of thinking, a good theorist gets nervous about whether my hours are really the Platonic ideal of the essence of thinking. In short, the result of describing how a number came to be generated is to make it appear a much more theoretical entity, and thereby much more uncertain as a fact, a much more precarious test of a theory. This in turn means that most numbers in history, more carelessly generated than this, from noncomparable instances, cannot serve the purpose that a positivist view of science assigns them. They too involve theory, not just facts.

But from the point of view of this book, a more important difficulty is that much of the potential theoretical illumination to be derived from a particular fact is already stripped from it in order to turn it into an instance to be counted. My argument here will be that the central operation for building theories of history is seeking causally significant analogies between instances. If the instances are immediately stripped of all features that would lead to new analogies (i.e., new concepts) in order to turn them into a count based on one of those analogies between the counted instances that we knew from the beginning, then one sacrifices from the first the capacity for theoretical innovation. A count should be the last stage of theoretically oriented social research, after one has got to the point where one is willing to sacrifice theoretical advance.

## EPOCHAL INTERPRETATIONS

Another subject that might reasonably be treated in a book with this title is the grand theory of history. When Marx, for example, summarizes a large number of changes in recent history as changes from a "feudal" mode of production to a "capitalist" mode of production, while Parsons treats those same changes as progressive differentiation, de

Jouvenel as the growth of "the powerhouse state," Duncan and Lieberson as successive types of urbanization, and a variety of people as "modernization," theoretically oriented historical research surely should have something to say about it.

But first we have to see what the question is to which these various concepts of historical change are directed. The idea behind all of them is that there is a master mechanism operating throughout long periods of history, whose effects are cumulative. The change from a mode of production in which a lord takes part of the product of a tenant plot (or receives labor dues on domain land) to one in which a capitalist buys labor at a market price and sells the product of that labor on the market for more money, is supposed to go on continuously from about the fifteenth century. It is supposed to have a continuous effect on the social organization of production (increasing the interdependence of workers and their use of machines, to culminate in the factory, increasing the relative weight of capitalist labor relations as opposed to feudal labor relations), an effect of creating a push toward bourgeois democratic political forms, an effect of concentrating the proletariat, and the like. This continuous process produces crises, such as the French Revolution, when the political prerequisites of the capitalist mode of production cannot be produced by a royal government permeated by feudal remnants.

De Jouvenel, in contrast, sees the power of government growing straight through the French Revolution, nothing being really different after than before in any essential respect. The cumulation over a long period is the growth of government power, again with the multiple effects in all areas of life and cumulative effects at least since the fifteenth century.

The question posed by these two alternative visions is whether there is any way to bring historical evidence to bear on the question of "What is mainly going on?" The main facts in both cases are clear: Rents from productive property let to workers were a much more important source of income for the rich in the fifteenth century than in the twentieth, and governments manage much more of the flow of national income, of the flow of people through school, through the labor market, and into retirement, of the flow of coercion and violence, in the twentieth century than in the fifteenth. In short, the facts support both Marx and de Jouvenel.

Likewise, the main facts interpreted by the other epochal theories are not in dispute: Institutions are more differentiated and specialized in the twentieth century than they were in the fifteenth; cities have evolved from commercial and governmental centers managing flows of agricultural goods, then to manufacturing centers, to providers of complex metropolitan services to a diversified and dispersed productive system; a large number of indicators of modernity, from education to urbanization to mass political participation, have moved together from the fifteenth century to the twentieth, with Western Europe, North and South America, and Australia–New Zealand leading and other countries moving in the same direction with lags.

If the main facts that each epochal theory interprets are not in dispute, what then is the conflict about? The conflict has to do with how these cumulations of effects over time come about. De Jouvenel conflicts with Marx about the nature of cumulative causation in politics. The debate is about whether, for example, the French Revolution changed the direction and nature of the growth of government regulation of society sufficiently to matter, with Marxists arguing that the movement after the Revolution was in a direction that preserved market positions of capitalists and preserved labor market mechanisms for extracting surplus value, and with de Jouvenel arguing that both before and after the Revolution governments did whatever would give the state maximum power—that for example bourgeois property was defended both before and after the Revolution if such defense increased tax revenues, increased supplies for the army, or increased support by the rich and powerful for the government.

The nature of this debate may become clearer if we restate it in the form made popular by econometric practice. The debate between Marxists and de Jouvenel is structurally equivalent to asking: Can the (long-run) system of structural equations describing the evolution of the system be restated in a reduced form in which changes in the mode of production (or changes in the power position of governments) are the only exogenous variables, without loss of relevant information? And then in turn, can the cumulative change of these exogenous variables be explained by mechanisms exclusively in the sector taken to be basic?

De Jouvenel is not arguing that the bourgeoisie do not have different notions of government from those of the nobility and that these do not affect the process of the Revolution. Instead, his argument is that whatever the rhetoric, whatever the class relations, what a historian needs to know to predict the outcome is what action will increase the power of the government. The rest of the mechanism—class conflict and everything else—is still there, but it does not give new information. The Marxist argument is the reverse, that capitalist property relations are sufficiently powerful causes to produce all the intermediate mechanisms necessary (including an increasingly powerful government) to create the conditions of its own reproduction.

Likewise, the modernism model maintains that in some rather vague way all one needs to know is at what level all the indicators of modernism were last year to know them all (with a margin of error) for this year, because modernism cumulates. For Parsons, if a half-century previously the institutions of theology and science were differentiated, it is likely that we will see signs of the differentiation of engineering and science, and of ethics and theology, and that we will not find engineering institutions differentiating from science before science is differentiated from theology; the crisis of the French Revolution in its ideological aspect may be resolved by differentiating the *philosophes* into atheist theologians, scientists, engineers, and writers on social policy, all in their separate institutions.

How can historical research bear on the question of whether a particular reduced form of a system of equations contains all the relevant information? It cannot be by remaining at the level of epochal facts, because all those facts move together from the fifteenth to the twentieth centuries. Consequently, it has to be in more detailed studies of particular historical sequences that evidence comes for deciding among epochal theories. As methods for summarizing the long sweep of history, then, epochal theories have merely literary functions. They are produced for the textbook function of historical writing, that of giving a specious sense that we understand the nature of the society we live in by providing a myth of how it came about—a myth illustrated with historical events.

But such a narrative structure for the long sweep can provide concepts for more detailed studies. Several of the books analyzed here get some of their concepts from long-sweep theories: Trotsky from Marxism; de Tocqueville from the progress of equality; Smelser from functional differentiation; Bendix from the rationalization and bureaucratization of the world. Our problem here is whether this matters, whether any of the researches bear on the question, "Which epochal theory is appropriate?" My answer is negative.

These monographs achieve the illusion of bearing on the epochal questions through verbal sleight of hand. There are two main literary devices involved, both using the apparent causal structure created by narrative of a sequence of events to create the illusion that epochal theories are being substantiated. The first is choosing portentous names, names from the epochal theories, for concepts actually defined in quite another way. Calling the Social Revolutionaries a "petty bourgeois party," implies that whatever that party does derives from the historical position of the petty bourgeoisie, even if no analysis of small businessmen's politics is done. (It is not done in Trotsky's *History of the Russian Revolution.*)

The second takes advantage of the literary fact that whatever one starts with appears as the cause of a narrative, and one starts historical books with a schematic account of the background to the narrative. It complements this with the fact that one ends with an assessment in schematic terms of what the whole business added up to, rather than a theoretical analysis of the logical character of the narrative. Thus the weakest part of the intellectual structure, from the point of view of causal evidence, appears in the literary form of a historical book as the summary cause in the introduction and the summary effect in the conclusion.

For example, I argue later that the central causal dynamics outlined in the empirical body of Trotsky's *History of the Russian Revolution* are the same as those advanced in de Tocqueville's *The Old Regime and the French Revolution*. A naive analysis leads readers (except Stalinists) to conclude that Trotsky's monograph contributes to the solidity of the Marxist view of history simply because it starts with a 15-page schematic history of Russia in Marxist terms—one of the masterpieces of the Marxist theory of history—and ends with an analysis of why Trotsky's policy rather than Stalin's represents the Marxist lessons of the Revolution. De Tocqueville starts with a picture of feudal independence being undermined by royal officials and ends with Louis XVI about to be overthrown and executed for his misdeeds. None of these schematic accounts of the beginning and end is carefully connected, with causally relevant evidence, to any of the events analyzed in the body of the book, except by naming the events properly. Thus the first device, causal analysis by naming, supplements the second.

For example, the tsar and the government are called feudal by Trotsky, royal (and implicitly antifeudal) by de Tocqueville. This does not mean that these two historians have a different analysis of why these governments fell—in fact my argument will be that they had the same theory. Nor does it mean that Trotsky did not understand the opposition of the nobles to the Tsarist government—he claims that without that opposition the Russian Revolution might not have happened (in a passage analyzed in Chapter 2). Nor does it mean that de Tocqueville did not know about the royal efforts to keep the feudal status system of the nobility straight by examining titles of bourgeois upstarts, for he uses quotations from the appropriate body, about the titles "having been obtained by surprise."

In short, Trotsky and de Tocqueville do not disagree on the main descriptions of the royal regime, only in the names chosen. The names make it appear that events that happen to the Russian regime fit into a epochal theory that has the proletariat fighting feudalism more effectively than the bourgeoisie did, while those that happen to the Old

Regime fit into a epochal theory in which the regime had foolishly eroded its feudal supports.

Similarly, Trotsky casually calling the Kadets a "bourgeois" party, when its leading figures were mainly government and military officials, contributes a specious Marxist epochal dimension to the conflict between Bolsheviks and Kadets.

This literary device is systematized by Smelser. Smelser develops the epochal theory explicitly as a system of names ("theoretical boxes"). This systematization produces a literary stiffness that makes the whole sleight of hand appear clumsy, as when the analysis by a Bolton spinner, with an identical theory of the difficulty of supervising children in the factory to that of Smelser himself, has to be called "disturbed" thinking, because that is where it has to fall in the epochal theory (see the analysis in Chapter 3).

Thus causes become apparently exogenous by appearing in thin analyses at the beginnings and endings and these beginnings and endings are linked to the historical evidence through a thematic unity imposed by calling causes appearing in the course of the narrative by epochal names. This is not what is needed to establish that the reduced form of a system of equations contains all the information contained by the whole system.

How then can we use detailed historical studies to explain why a large number of variables, from the proportion of rents of productive property in property income to literacy rates, cumulate over five centuries? Which causal processes are inherently cumulative and cause the cumulation of the rest? I do not think we are near to being able to answer this question, but the general nature of the answer I advocate informs the strategy of this book. Briefly, the first step is to construct for particular cumulative processes—such as political evolution from 1917 to 1920 in Russia, or the evolution of working-class family institutions outside the factory from 1790 to 1840 in England—a theory that is causally adequate to the cumulation. In order to speak to the epochal question at all, the theory has to be of a form that explains the systematic evolution of institutions over reasonably large segments of time.

Then from these detailed analyses, those forces that appear exogenous for a particular development (e.g., the inability of the officers of a defeated army to command in 1918; the growth of the size of the crew for a spinning mule) have to be taken as the dependent variables in a second stage of theory building. By successively pushing through the equations until we can push no farther, we come to exogenous variables.

But this means that books with epochal pretensions have to be cut down to size, shorn of their narrative structure to get at their causal structure, before we can address the epochal questions that now get specious answers. It is to this preliminary task of tossing out the epochal garbage to get at the causal core of the studies that my analysis here is directed.

## THE THEORETICAL CHARACTER OF NARRATIVE

Another question the reader might expect to be addressed is the theoretical status of the main tool of the historian, a narrative of a sequence of events. Most language in everyday life is used either to evaluate a fact as good or bad (usually achieved with adjectives or nouns), or as a causal statement to aid in manipulation of the world (usually achieved with verbs or adjectives). As the professional tone has taken over history (from the praising and damning tone of chronicles), the normal linguistic effect is to make the narrative *appear* causal. The infinite narrative sequence of causes, making anything into a historical entity with a unique causal composition, is what makes Nietzsche believe that historical entities are not graspable by general concepts. The infinitely branching tree of causal sequences, rendered unified in a narrative of a sequence giving a unique explanation for each concrete historical entity, looks queer from the point of view of generalizing social science theory.

As implied in the Preface, my purpose here is to save the correct perception in this view from the pernicious philosophy of history in which it is embedded. I have picked for study monographs that have theoretical aspirations; and I have theoretical aspirations. I have no interest in patching together the sequence of causes—personal, social, and situational—that led to Stalin being on top at the end of the Russian Revolution and Napoleon at the end of the French. With proper guidance from *The 18th Brumaire*, I am interested in "Bonapartism," a more or less detailed analogy between the historical sources, bases of support, and historical effect of Napoleon and Louis Napoleon. I might possibly be convinced that the analogy of these two to Stalin was sufficiently close to be a productive theoretical starting point (at the present time, I am not convinced); but what interests me is Bonapartism, not Stalin or Napoleon or Louis Bonaparte.

Yet all the books I choose to analyze are narratives of a sequence of events, and this choice is central to my argument. I believe the test of any theory of social change is its ability to analyze such narrative sequences, and that the poverty of the theory of social change is due to paying no attention to that narrative detail. The problem here is to break narrative from its naive epistemological moorings, from the impression that the narrative is a causal theory because the tone of the language of narrative is causal, and so to make it useful for social theory. This does not mean that I am personally not interested in the story of history; it only means that for the purpose of advancing causal understanding, the unique sequence that brought Stalin to power has to be broken up into theoretically understandable bits. When those bits get back into the narrative, having been theoretically interpreted, the narrative will also be improved by being grounded in general ideas. But if it is grounded in general ideas at the level of the sequence as a whole, those ideas will be flaccid epochal notions with little capacity for illumination.

Let us go into a bit more logical detail. A certain event occurs, such as Trotsky leading the military coup that put the Bolsheviks in power in Petersburg. As a part of the Trotskyist narrative of the origin of Stalinism, this serves the chronicler function of showing our man Trotsky as a hero, trusted by Lenin, head of the Petrograd Soviet and the Military Revolutionary Committee, and thus selected by the masses to lead their revolution. It is hard to find out what these facts mean in the Stalinist narrative, because they do not appear there. If one wants to know about the unique sequence of events, the fact then appears as part of a story of betrayal of the Revolution, held together by moral themes.

The actual causal problem is much more delicate. This event is an element of a class of events in which a party oriented toward a coup d'etat, as represented by Lenin, can only carry it out through organs designed to represent the poor of Petersburg, and consequently only by operating through the leader of those organs, namely Trotsky. Trotsky is much more concerned than Lenin with maintaining the consent of these organs to the coup, and so postpones the coup over Lenin's objections. The general problem here is the relation between executive organs (the military committee) legitimated by populist devices, and representative organs (the Soviets) that are the formal source of that legitimation. What is required to win is a military act which has not been, and might not be, approved by the Soviets; further, this act has to be carried out more or less in secret, or troops will be called back from the front to stop it. This causal texture of the act makes it, in different degrees, analogous to acts of the CIA out of the control of the American Congress, analogous to the alternation of usual trade-union populist practices (with infinite debate) to tightly disciplined strike strategy committees, analogous to elected Southern state governments getting their states into the Civil War in 1861 in spite of the precarious popular legitimacy of that war. None of these analogous situations led to anything comparable to Stalin beating out Trotsky in a succession fight in which revolutionary purity was a central issue. Though they were parts of a different narrative sequence, anyone of them can be illuminated by analogies with the others. The analogy, hence the concept, is at the level of a particular part of the sequence, not that of the sequence as a whole.

But what do we need to know to see the analogy? That in the concrete historical sequence, the Bolshevik party had come to be simultaneously an executive agency oriented toward a coup and the leading party in a set of populist institutions that might legitimate a coup. This sequence consisted of particular conflicts over revolutionary policy within the Central Committee of the Bolshevik party, and shifts in popular opinion and in participation of representatives in the Petersburg Soviet. The contrasting lines of development in the two types of bodies produced subsections in the Party that were differently oriented to the problems of the coup, namely those more concerned with popular legitimacy and those more concerned with executive efficiency. These were not inherent in the Party from the first (quite a different conflict, over whether to have a coup or not, was a permanent structural feature of the Party). The meaning of this element in the sequence, the part that gives evidence of the analogy, is the narrative of the conflict between Lenin and Trotsky over the date of the coup, because it is only there that the reasons Trotsky had for postponing (legitimacy) and that Lenin had for hurrying (effective action) came out.

Regardless of the validity of Trotsky's narrative (he is partly defending himself against an accusation that he opposed the coup for social-democratic reasons), the logical point is clear. The analogy between this particular segment of the narrative sequence and, say, the planning of the Southern insurrection by elected officials of Southern states, cannot be based on the narrative sequence as a whole. The narrative background (e.g., legitimate elected governments rather than Soviets), the long-term consequences (defeat for the South, Stalinism for the Soviet Union), and the purposes of the insurrection (defending versus attacking upper class privileges) were different.

What is the purpose then of making the analogy at all, when the historic significance is so different? Is the "real reality" not the difference in overall historical sources and consequences, in the uniqueness of the narrative sequences, rather than a patchwork of analogies between bits and pieces of the sequences? The answer, for the purposes of this book, is that the larger narrative is irrelevant. There are many other purposes for which the narrative is important. If one wanted to "explain Stalinism," one would need the important elements of the narrative sequence—for example, Stalin's and Trotsky's interpretations of what Trotsky was up to and of whether it challenged his revolutionary purity. But if one is instead interested in a "theory of authority in representative systems in revolutions," one needs to break out the relevant part of the narrative.

But this in its turn does *not* mean that one should ignore the narrative, because that is where the evidence on the causal nature of this part of the sequence comes from, and where its causal influence can be judged. Nor does it mean that a person concerned with the whole narrative should ignore such piece-by-piece generalizing impulses. This is where Nietzsche's aphorism goes wrong. (Nietzsche himself does not follow his own advice in his historical work.)

For the selection of aspects of the sequence as a whole that need to be reported rests on a causal understanding of each of the links in the sequence. Trotsky and Lenin were not just being erratic individuals in this situation, but instead were in positions in the flow of events that generally produce similar conflicts. A narrative that selects out "Trotsky, as leader of the Party in the Soviet and chairman of the Soviet's Military Revolutionary Committee, conflicted ... "rather than, say, "Trotsky, whose adherence to the Bolshevik party came late in his career, conflic- ted ...," is more causally adequate as narrative because it recognizes the causal sources of this link in the sequence. The second quotation col- lapses the debate which was to occur later between Stalin and Trotsky into a part of the sequence in which it has, as far as I can tell, no causal business. The collapsing may improve the literary effect, but not the contribution to understanding of the narrative of the origins of Stalinism. It is a close relative of "Little did Marie Antoinette know as she donned her silk dress...."

The main mistake of the grand theory of social change is that it tries to make analogies (i.e., to invent concepts—later in this chapter I treat why these are logically equivalent) at the level of the large narrative of overall sequences: The French Revolution leads to Napoleon as the Russian Revolution leads to Stalin; or, even grander: "Feudalism leads to a bourgeois revolution which leads to a proletarian revolution." It is such reckless theorizing that has got theory a bad name among historians and other knowledgeable people; the reason it is bad is that it has to ignore most of the facts in order to get its concepts going. It is not necessary to ignore the facts in order to have general concepts, as the example of the physical sciences shows. The argument of this book is that it is not only not necessary, it is also a bad idea.

## THE INTELLECTUAL TRADITION AND THIS BOOK

This introduction might be misinterpreted as an apology for not having written a book that might naturally be expected from the title. My reason for titling the book in a way that makes the body of the book seem odd is that I really think it is more on the subject of the title than the book one might expect. My first job, from a rhetorical point of view, is to try to convince the reader that the image of the question of social theory in history that he or she had in mind, that led him or her to pick up a book with this title, is the wrong question. It is the wrong question because people do much better theory when interpreting the historical sequence than they do when they set out to do "theory"; and the reason for that fact is that our idea of what theory ought to do for us is shaped by a mistaken epistemology given to us by the positivists, a mistaken idea of what a fact is given to us by quantifiers, a mistaken idea of how narrative relates to causation given to us by a combination of the semantic structures of narrative matter-of-fact English and mistaken philosophies of history.

I hope that this argument has not yet been convincing, because the guts of the argument are the analysis of historical monographs in the book itself. But given my purposes, as explained in the preceding sections, I should be expected to give evidence from the monographs for the following points:

1. That concepts other than epochal concepts appear in these monographs, and that these concepts are general concepts
2. That the most fruitful of these concepts are invented by detailed examination of the analogies between historical instances
3. That the same general concepts appear in the causal explanations of historical events given by theorists with different epochal theories
4. That the same general concepts occur in the detailed analyses of different historical sequences, sequences that had different ultimate origins and different ultimate consequences. Causation does not operate at the grand level of "Why did the Russian Revolution lead to Stalinism?" but on the segmented level of "How do revolutionary legislatures legitimate coups d'etat?"

## LOGIC, CLASSES, AND CAUSAL STATEMENTS

The logical character of the argument of this book is extremely simple. It is that every concept (e.g., a logical class) can be described either by its predicates (e.g., "corporately organized" and "distributing status unequally") or by the set of equivalences among the elements (e.g., "society A and society B both require people to carry out celebrations of marriage in the presence of a large group of members of the community"). The analogy between society $A$ and society $B$ in marriage practices makes them both corporately organized groups. This implies that any causal statement such as "all corporately organized groups of people distribute status unequally" can be restated in the form, "Every set of people who are analogous to another set of people in corporate legitimation of marriage are also analogous in distributing rewards and duties unequally." Corporate legitimation of marriage is, of course, only one of the many analogies between instances which are included in the predicate, corporately organized, and it is probably not the crucial one.

All societies are, of course, corporately organized groups; and so Soviet society is. If the causal generalization in the preceding paragraph were taken as true, it would follow that Soviet society distributes status unequally. The logic here follows the pattern of, "All men are mortal; Socrates is a man; therefore Socrates is mortal." Further, "All societies are corporately organized," together with "All corporately organized groups distribute status unequally," by classical logic leads to "All societies distribute status unequally." The same pattern of reasoning leads to "All firms distribute status unequally," or to "General Motors distributes status unequally."

We want to ask here whether the substance involved in the predicate, "corporately organized," is sufficient to explain why General Motors and the Soviet Union behave, in certain respects, alike. What does that substance consist of? And in particular, how are social scientists to conduct their research in such a way as to move successfully from generalizations of the form "All societies distribute status unequally" to "All corporately organized groups distribute status unequally," if it is indeed true that the causes of unequal distribution of status lie in corporate organization rather than in being a society.

The argument will be that it is often more fruitful to ask oneself questions of the form "What similarity between General Motors and the Soviet Union accounts for their both allocating rewards and duties unequally?" than to ask it in the form "What is the most general predicate $g$, for which the generalization is true, if $x$ is a $g$, then $x$ distributes status unequally?" When we find the consequential analogies between General Motors and the Soviet Union, many of them will be elements of the predicate $g$. (Many will not, of course: The fact that they took their present constitutional forms, in their major outlines, during the 1920s is an analogy between General Motors and the Soviet Union that presumably is irrelevant to their unequal allocation of status.)

Since the two methods of looking for analogies between cases of interest and looking for predicates of a class of interest logically are exactly equivalent, we can use either method in our hunt for concepts. If we have a causally interesting class, such as groups that distribute status unequally, we can try a predicate on one instance of that class after another until we come to an instance to which the predicate does not apply and then change the predicate, or we can study the analogy between the first and second instance, see how much of that holds up as an analogy between the first and third, and so on.

Let us turn to a more concrete example of Trotsky developing a concept describing political parties, which classified Bolsheviks together with the Kadets (a "bourgeois-democratic" party) in contrast to the Social Revolutionaries (a "peasant" party—the party of the head of the Provisional Government, Kerensky).

## A CASE OF ANALOGY

In Chapter 2, I analyze the microsociology used in two books whose object is to explain a concrete sequence of events: Leon Trotsky's *History of the Russian Revolution* (1932) and Alexis de Tocqueville's *The Old Regime and the French Revolution* (1856). [1] By *microsociology* I mean approximately what Trotsky means when he speaks of "molecular processes," the constituent human thoughts and actions (and their causes) which make up collective or structural outcomes.

Consider, for example, Trotsky's characterization of the Social Revolutionary party early in 1917. He has just explained that those who wanted a capitalist, limited franchise regime and continuation of the war voted for the Kadets, those who wanted socialism and peace voted for the Bolsheviks, while everyone else voted Social Revolutionary.

> A party for whom everybody votes except that minority who know what they are voting for, is no more a party, than the tongue in which babies of all countries babble is a national language [*HRR* I, p. 223.].

Aside from that seductive literary grace which allows Trotsky to suggest that the Social Revolutionaries are babbling without his having to say and hence defend it, what is going on in this passage? He is suggesting that the constituent loyalties that make up the Kadet and Bolshevik parties are of a different kind from those making up the Social Revolutionary party. Hence we will expect various causal forces (sum-

---

[1] I refer to these books as *HRR* and *ORR*, respectively, and to other books frequently quoted by their initials. Bibliographical details are given in the references.

med up as the progress of the revolution) to have different effects on the reactionary and radical parties than on the loose, rhetorical, populist coalition of the Social Revolutionaries.

I have chosen this case to show that the concepts need be neither mysterious nor profound to generate a good deal of light. Here Trotsky is making an analogy between the right-wing party and his own (left, of course) party. Clearly, being who he is, he is unlikely to make such an analogy for purposes of persuading Bolsheviks to be Kadets or to steal honor from the Kadets for the Bolsheviks, so it must have an explanatory purpose. The purpose is to explain why the Social Revolutionaries could not hold power and govern, why their support faded away during the revolution while that of both the Kadets and the Bolsheviks increased (relatively, at least), why this largest party split down the middle during the course of the revolution, leaving its leaders in the government stranded on the highest peak with no way to get down to influence events, why the October Revolution found none of the masses ready to defend the Social Revolutionary government the masses had created. The analogy is elaborated at various points in the book, almost casually, as if it were a literary game, so that we end up with a deep symmetry between the Bolsheviks and Kadets and come to expect them to behave alike and to expect their historian (Miliukov, the Kadet foreign minister) to have the same sort of contempt for the center politicians as Trotsky had.

But what does this deep analogy consist of? I want to talk here from a mechanical or formal point of view, so as to be able to see, whenever possible, an analogy between the method of Trotsky and that of de Tocqueville that goes beyond their common contempt for petty bourgeois "enlightened" intellectuals. I therefore cannot say that it comes from the correctness of the general Marxist–Leninist conception, which obviously would have horrified de Tocqueville. (Nor can I conversely, of course, say that it is due to de Tocqueville realizing that feudalism was true freedom, so that everything since is to be judged by the degree of its corruption from that pristine state).

Concretely, the analogy between parties consists of the actions of people or, more exactly, the causal texture of their actions. It is the similarity in the cause of the vote (namely, understanding the kind of society being advocated by the Party, wanting that kind, and being willing to pay some price for it) that causes the Kadets and Bolsheviks to be analogous and different from the Social Revolutionaries. It is these microsociological bases of analogy between concrete collective events, trends, and structures that I want to analyze in the first section, using Trotsky and de Tocqueville as examples.

Since it will soon become obvious to the reader anyway, let me warn him here that I much prefer Trotsky. Part of that preference is political: I think that both the French and the Russian revolutions were on balance good things; de Tocqueville clearly disagrees about the one he had a chance to judge, and I think no one would seriously doubt how he would react to the Russian Revolution. Part of it is stylistic: Trotsky forgets political rationality for his movement whenever he gets a chance at elegantly expressed intellectual contempt; this is a corrupt taste of my own. But I hope to show, incidentally to my main purpose, that it is in part because de Tocqueville was a sloppier thinker, making analogies he did not really believe when it suited the flow of the argument and generally showing less theoretical self-discipline.

## EXPLICATION

Classifying $A$ and $B$ together is, in a science, an empirical assertion. It says that there is a consequential analogy between $A$ and $B$. Logically, any class is a statement that, for all the pairs of members of the class, and for a (large) series of general statements made about the class, element $A$ is analogous to element $B$, $B$ analogous to $C$, $A$ to $C$, $A$ to $D$, etc. That is, a class is a set of pairwise equivalence relations, among the elements of the class, with respect to the predicates that apply to the class. We would, in ordinary language, say that the analogy between $A$ and $D$ was a *"deep"* analogy, if a great many statements true of $A$ are also true of $D$. A class in which the equivalences are deep analogies is an important concept. In a science, if these statements are of an important causal character, the concept is important.

But if general concepts consist in the analogies between elements and if they are deeper if the analogies are deeper, then the basic investigatory task of concept formation is the deepening analogies. Far from it being the case that the most powerful general theorists ignore the details, the precise opposite is true. Social theory without attention to details is wind; the classes it invents are vacuous, and nothing interesting follows from the fact that $A$ and $B$ belong to the class; "theoretical" research appears as a species of wordy scholasticism, arranging conceptual angels in sixteenfold ranks on the head of a purely conceptual pin.

But if conceptual profundity depends on the deep building of analogies from one case to another, we are likely to find good theory in exactly the opposite place from where we have been taught to expect it. For it is likely to be those scholars who attempt to give a *causal interpreta-*

*tion of a particular case* who will be led to penetrate the deeper analogies between cases. And this I believe we find the case in the literature of sociology. As Hugh Stretton (1969) has said:

> [Talcott Parsons] gambles for general truth by the method of insisting on the generality, then seeing what truths can be found there. If sufficiently useful truths were found, they might indeed be more powerful than anybody else's [p. 293].

But the consequence we should draw from Parsons' failure is not to return to untheoretical science but instead to return to the strategy that originally inspired Parsons, that of Max Weber. Parsons was deceived about where the power of Weber's theory came from. It was exactly *not* in classifying together all things vaguely like capitalism as *universalism*, exactly by piecemeal deepening of analogies, that Weber becomes so exciting.

The purpose of this essay in historical method is not, however, to provide a dictionary of deep analogies which students of historical materials have developed. The first part of Weber's *Wirtschaft und Gesellschaft* does this (translated first, significantly enough in the light of his later misapprehension about how to do theoretical work, with Parsons' participation), and is deadly dull as a consequence. There is hardly any intellectual adventure in a dictionary, though it is one way to classify the historical deposit of what has been said in a language. Likewise there is little intellectual adventure in Weber's dictionary of sociological concepts.

I argue, however, that there is intellectual adventure in contrasting the Bolsheviks and the Kadets to the Social Revolutionaries. It is similar to the adventure in *The Protestant Ethic* where Weber tries to see whether the things that differentiate Quakers from Calvinists are essential to his purpose—will Quakers develop the spirit of capitalism without a transcendental God? The analogy built up between the Kadets and the Bolsheviks is deep because it is an analogy between the actions and sentiments of followers of the Party. In social science, such analogies yield rich concepts that fruitfully enter into many causal statements. If two movements have the same elementary components of action and sentiment, while another movement is different from both in the kinds of actions and sentiments that make it up, the shocks of the Revolution will deal with the two kinds of movements very differently. The concept invented by careful comparison of what actions and sentiments made up three parties is, then, a causally profound concept.

## HISTORY IN MODERN SOCIOLOGY

In Chapter 3 I want to undertake a more contentious task, to show that when they are really good, really illuminating, modern social scientists do not in fact do their theoretical work in the way we, as a profession, claim to do it. That is, I will argue that the general theory from which particular analyses are supposed, in our epistemological discussions, to be derived is too vacuous to derive anything interesting from, and that *when* sociologists *do* start (mistakenly) deriving historical sequences from general theory seriously, we can still see the historical picture move, but it is all blurry, like a school movie run by a beginning projectionist. But when, reading a book on social change, we strike a passage or an argument that seems crisp and interesting, when the figures on the screen take on temporary definition as the projectionist by accident temporarily hits on the correct focus, the concepts out of which the picture is built are laboriously constructed deep analogies, generally of the same kind that the more historian-like Trotsky or de Tocqueville also use.

Finding work on social change by sociologists with theoretical aspirations, which was good enough to manifest this contrast in method in different parts of the work, was a serious problem. I have chosen to analyze Reinhard Bendix's *Work and Authority in Industry* and Neil Smelser's *Social Change in the Industrial Revolution*. Bendix, I suppose, falls neatly halfway between the unequivocal historical commitments of the previous authors and Smelser's unequivocal interest in developing general theory. Bendix is deeply suspicious of the facile character of modern social theory, but he cannot resist it. Though perhaps he feels seduced by his muse rather than inspired by her, he writes essays on general concepts such as "bureaucracy" and "power" or "tradition" and "modernity," if sometimes only to express suspicion. Smelser, on the other hand, is capable of theoretical leaps on a grand scale; this inspires in me so much fellow feeling that I hate to write an essay about our common faults.

## EMPIRICISM AND THEORETICAL STRATEGIES

Presumably by now the reader has the idea that this essay is to be an empiricist diatribe, an essay about how "facts" are superior to "speculation." And no doubt to some extent that is right. But the character of the argument is not, logically speaking, one about the ancient epistemological question of facts being true, and being the means by which we see whether theories are true. That is, it is not about the traditional epistemological question of verifiability, and of why science based on facts is better than theology based on speculation. Instead it is about the use of facts to *improve* ideas, to make them richer, more flexible, more powerful.

Let us return to Trotsky and the Social Revolutionary party. The traditional, *epistemological*, way of analyzing this passage either would be that

1. This is a general hypothesis (*a*) at the "molecular" level, about the class of acts of voting for the Social Revolutionaries as opposed to the class of acts of voting Bolshevik or Kadet, and (*b*) at the level of political parties, about the set of historical circumstances in which the Social Revolutionary party will decay or split while the Bolsheviks and Kadets hang together—what we need to know about these generalizations is whether they are true or not, and what we need to know about Trotsky's work is whether he has provided us with evidence or facts to test these generalizations.

Or an alternative explication of Trotsky's passage would be that

2. This is a factual observation which classifies Social Revolutionaries into one class, Kadets and Bolsheviks into another, so as to render further factual observations about these parties *relevant to* a generalization about, say, what tends to happen to populist parties as opposed to parties organized around a serious class program—what we need to know about Trotsky is whether he is reporting this classifying fact correctly, and using it responsibly to test the generalization about populism.

There are of course very worthwhile questions. It is the fact that these questions are *both* so interesting that convinces me that the passage is an important piece of social science, rather than a merely literary device to keep the narrative moving by fixing the parties to the drama in the reader's mind. But these two questions are not the questions I am interested in addressing here. Instead I want to know *how did Trotsky use the facts to arrive at such interesting questions?*

The basic idea behind the answer I will try to give to this question is that *fruitfulness* of the assertion, "elements $A$ and $B$ are members of the class $X$, rather than members of the class $Y$ (which has no members in common with $X$), " depends not on the resounding quality of the word associated with $X$ (such as *class party* versus *populist party*), but on the profundity of the equivalence relation, $A = B$. The more we form our concepts such as *class party* from detailed processual or causal similarity between *A* and *B*, between Kadets and Bolsheviks for example, the more interesting causal statements will these concepts enter into.

This is actually a tautological statement, for "detailed processual and causal similarity" is simply another way of saying "the common class predicated of the elements enters into many (true) causal statements." But as very often happens with tautologies, different forms of stating the same thing have different intuitive value, and therefore different usefulness to the practical investigator. If one knows two angles in a triangle and wants the third, the fact that the angles add up to 180 degrees is a more useful way of stating the axioms of Euclid, even though it is tautologously derived from them. I want to analyze the strategies of theory construction in these "historical" works from the point of view of deriving a general list of *strategic ways in which instances can be analogous*, and consequently strategic ways of building conceptual systems in research on social change.[2]

## TECHNICAL APPENDIX: THE LOGIC OF ANALOGY

Let us presume we have three objects, say General Motors, the Soviet Union, and the set of pedestrians visible from State and Madison at 1:10 PM on some chosen Friday. Intuitively, it is clear that the first two are corporate groups, that part of their corporate activity involves allocating rewards and duties to members, and that they do this unequally. While no doubt our pedestrians are unequal, that inequality is hardly a stratification system that pertains to sidewalks near State and Madison. We therefore have the intuitive feeling that if we could understand why

[2]I might mention how these particular works got selected. I started with a larger group of studies of a generally historical character of which I had thought intuitively, when I read them, that they were first rate. Besides the ones to be analyzed, they included several books by Clifford Geertz and one by E. J. Hobsbawm, Edmund Leach's *Political Systems of Highland Burma*, and Charles Tilly's *The Vendée*. As I tried to come to grips with the problem, these books got eliminated for different reasons. With Leach, it was because the tedious connections between the facts as observed and the theoretical interpretation have disappeared from the book, leaving me helpless in the analysis. With Tilly, it is because he is a highly self conscious sociological worker, and explains as well as I could the logic of his procedure. With Hobsbawn and especially Geertz, it seemed to me beyond my capacities to give an adequate account of what was going on. Geertz and Trotsky are perhaps in the same intellectual class, but I have lived with Trotsky and the tradition out of which he comes for over 20 years, so I feel I know what is going on in his mind that produces my bedazzlement. I have no advice about how to produce the bedazzlements that Geertz or Hobsbawm produce.

General Motors and the Soviet Union act alike in creating inequality, it might be causally solid knowledge of stratification, while the inequalities of the pedestrians come from so many sources that no one causal statement is likely to grasp them all. When Erving Goffman (1963) teaches us about the stratification of the pedestrians, the processes are mostly those of bleeding status from elsewhere into the signs one gives off as one walks near State and Madison.

Let our three objects be called $X_1$, $X_2$, and $X_3$. Then there are a set of predicate variables, $P$, which can be used to describe such objects. For example, the first predicate variable might be $P_{1j} =$ "does (or does not) the object $j$ have collective production of goods and services?" $P_{2j}$ might be "does (or does not) object $j$ have designated officials or written norms to admit people as members?" $P_{3j}$ might be, "Do some people in the group eat more protein than others?"

For these three variables, then, General Motors would have the values (does produce, does admit members, does have inequality of protein intake), the Soviet Union would have the same three values, and the pedestrians would have the values (does not produce, does not have formal membership, does have inequality of protein intake). Or in more abstract notation, letting the first subscript be the variable number and the second the object number, we would have

$$P_1 = (p_{11}, p_{21}, p_{31}, \ldots)$$
$$P_2 = (p_{12}, p_{22}, p_{32}, \ldots)$$
$$P_3 = (p_{13}, p_{23}, p_{33}, \ldots)$$

where

$p_{11} = p_{12} =$ does produce;
$p_{13} =$ does not produce;
$p_{21} = p_{22} =$ does have formal members;
$p_{23} =$ does not have formal members;
$p_{31} = p_{32} = p_{33} =$ does have inequality of protein intake.

Then $P_1$ is the set of all the predicates that apply to $X$ (to General Motors), $P_2$ is all those that apply to $X_2$ (to the Soviet Union), and $P_3$ is all those that apply to the pedestrians at State and Madison.

The *analogy* between $X_1$ and $X_2$ is the set of predicates they have in common, in this case all the first three (but not, for example, $P_{4j} =$ does object $j$ divide profits in proportion to investments?). The *differentiation* between $X_1$ and $X_3$ is the set of predicates on which they have different values, in this case the first two ($p_{11} \neq p_{13}$; $p_{21} \neq p_{23}$; but $p_{31} = p_{33}$).

The concept that divides $X_1$ and $X_2$ into one class, and $X_3$ into another, is the set of predicates which simultaneously are members of the analogy between $X_1$ and $X_2$ and of the differentiation (of either) from $X_3$. Or in more formal terms,

$$A_{12} = P_1 \cap P_2.$$

(Read, "The analogy between objects 1 and 2 is the intersection of the sets of predicates applying to each.")

$$A_{13} = P_1 \cap P_3.$$
$$D_{13} = P_3 - P_1 \cap P_3.$$

(Read, "The differentiation of objects 1 and 3 is all predicates that apply to them except those they have in common.")

$$_{12}C_3 = A_{12} \cap D_{13}.$$

(Read: "The concept differentiating objects 1 and 2 from object 3 is the set of predicates 1 and 2 have in common (their analogy) on which object 3 has a different value.")

The general objective of developing concepts is to form interesting sentences. In a science we want interesting *causal* sentences. We will leave *causal* undefined here except to specify that it has to do with the applicability of predicates to an object at some time in the future.[3]

Suppose in particular we want to assert something like: "All corporately organized groups distribute status unequally." Since, while the pedestrians eat different amounts of protein, they do not have the money to buy meat distributed by fellow pedestrians, we might say the set of pedestrians did not distribute status unequally (this is an implicit definition of "to distribute status." People will be treated differently on the street according to their age, race, physical condition, dress, etc. (see Goffman, 1963). Whether we want to call this "distributing status" is a purely verbal matter. If we do so, then we have to change the verb in the generalization to read something like "distribute status by collective decisions carried out by an administrative staff." Let us call this new predicate $g_1$, having the values "distributes status unequally" and "does not distribute status unequally, though it may recognize status distributed elsewhere."

If we take the definition of "to distribute status unequally" as given, in such a way that $X_1$ and $X_2$ have it and $X_3$ does not, then for the proposition to be true all the predicates involved in "corporately organized" must be in the set that we have defined as the concept that

[3]This does not mean that I think the only "test" of a scientific theory is prediction. Many theories are easily disproved by disproving logical implications which have nothing to do with future, however the future is defined.

divides $X_1$ and $X_2$ from $X_3$. Of course many predicates other than those involved in "corporately organized" will be in that set differentiating General Motors and the Soviet Union from the pedestrians, such as "took on their present constitutional form in the 1920s." The causally significant group of predicates will therefore be a subset of the predicates involved in the analogy between General Motors and the Soviet Union, which differentiate them from the group of pedestrians near State and Madison.

We can define the "causal fruitfulness" of the concept that differentiates objects $X_1$ and $X_2$ from $X_3$ as the set of all predicates that make causally interesting sentences ("predictions") with the concept. That is, the causal fruitfulness constitutes the respects in which the futures of General Motors and the Soviet Union are alike, and it tells us how much causal guts there is in the analogy we have formed between them.

But we want our concepts to be not only fruitful, but also economical. That is, if having their present constitution formed in the 1920s is irrelevant to a large part of the causal fruitfulness of the analogy, then we want to aim for a concept like "corporately organized" rather than one like "corporately organized in basically the same way since the 1920s," yet for some part of that causal fruitfulness (e.g., "distributes status unequally"), it would be a mistake to go as far as "social order" defined as "a set of actions of people in which there is a positive probability that any one action will be oriented in its course by taking account of another action," for that would include the pedestrians at State and Madison.

Reducing the analogy between two objects (in contrast to at least one other) to its scientifically relevant predicates requires scientific work. Some of that work can be theoretical, provided we have some "regulatory generalizations" that tell us some predicates are more likely than others. For instance, in social science we may generally assert that "concepts involving the interactions and judgments of people are usually more economical (for the same causal fruitfulness) than those involving impulses, instincts, or mechanical responses to stimuli."

But the basic source of information for stripping away irrelevancy from an analogy is the examination of new cases. If constitution-forming during the 1920s is crucial for having a status system, then the king of France in the eighteenth century will not hand out patents of nobility. If mutual consciousness and mutual orientation is sufficient to affect status, then people should change their lifetime expectations of rewards and duties while walking near State and Madison. That is, moving from an analogy between two things to an analogy (or differentiation) between three or more whose futures are, in the relevant respects, the same, is the main way to "deepen" an analogy. An analogy is deeper: (a) the more the futures of two objects are alike, that is, the larger the number of predicates involving the future that are analogous; (b) the more causally irrelevant parts of the analogy have been stripped away, that is, the more other objects equivalent to these two in the respects mentioned have similar futures.

It should be obvious that everything said here about deep analogies could equally well be said about deep predicates. In fact, we have carried along the predicate, "corporately organized," while outlining the analogy between General Motors and the Soviet Union, to communicate intuitively what the analogy of those two objects was really all about. The argument of this book is that this formal logical equivalence between an analogy between two objects and a (set of) predicate(s) defining a class can be used strategically.

Descartes' proof that algebra and geometry were really the same thing allows us to proceed either algebraically or geometrically, as suits our convenience. Likewise, the equivalence of analogies and predicates allows our theory building to proceed either by causally significant analogies or by generalizations about classes. Our argument is that in historical studies it is often more strategic to work by analogies.

# 2

# Analogy and Generality in Trotsky and de Tocqueville

## THE SOCIOLOGICAL BIAS
## OF TROTSKY AND DE TOCQUEVILLE

Both Trotsky and de Tocqueville conceived of their tasks as tasks of sociology, rather than of psychology or the mere reporting of the sequence of events. Trotsky states it most forcefully, if most contentiously, when introducing a discussion of the psychology of the tsar and his family and entourage.

> This book will concern itself least of all with those unrelated psychological researches which are now so often substituted for social and historical analysis. Foremost in our field of vision will stand the great, moving forces of history, which are super-personal in character. Monarchy is one of them. But all these forces operate through people. And monarchy is by its very principle bound up with the personal. . . . Moreover, we hope to show in what follows, partially at least, just where in a personality the strictly personal ends—often much sooner than we think—and how frequently the "distinguishing traits" of a person are merely scratches made by a higher law of development [HRR, I, p. 52].

Or with perhaps more literary effect, the following passage:

Some professional psychologist ought to draw up an anthology of the parallel expressions of Nicholas and Louis, Alexandra and Antoinette, and their courtiers... the result would be a highly instructive historic testimony in favor of the materialist psychology. Similar (of course, far from identical) irritations in similar conditions call out similar reflexes; the more powerful the irritation, the sooner it overcomes personal peculiarities. To a tickle, people react differently, but to a redhot iron alike. As a steam-hammer converts a sphere and a cube alike into sheet metal, so under the blow of too great and inexorable events resistances are smashed and the boundaries of "individuality" are lost [HRR, I, p.93].

Not only does Trotsky take a strong position on the relative role of individual characteristics as opposed to social characteristics, but he takes a very strong position on where social characteristics come from—not from a sort of social deposit in the lives of individuals, whence then the causal force comes, but rather from the network of social relations itself. In refuting Tseretelli, a socialist minister who had said "It is impossible to deny, especially at such a moment, the great relative weight... of those who are strong through the possession of property," Trotsky replies:

But the whole point was that this weight was becoming more and more impossible to weigh. Just as weight is not an inner attribute of individual objects, but an interrelation between them, so social weight is not a natural property of people but only that class attribute which other classes are compelled to recognize in them. The revolution, however, had come right up to the point where it was refusing to recognize this most fundamental "attribute" of the ruling classes. It was for this reason that the position of the eminent minority on the short arm of the lever [i.e., the right wing] was becoming so uncomfortable [HRR, II, p. 177].

De Tocqueville does not quite so explicitly take a radically sociological position, but it is clear from his general strategy as outlined in the following passage that he is very little interested in accidental qualities of individuals.

In fact, my method has been that of the anatomist who dissects each defunct organ [of the Old Regime] with a view to eliciting the laws of life, and my aim has been to supply a picture that while scientifically accurate, may also be instructive [ORR, p. xii].

Thus, although the intellectual purpose of both monographs is the interpretation of concrete historical sequences, both men take the view that such understanding is basically a scientific rather than a historical task, and that the science needed is sociological.

## THE SOCIOLOGY OF AUTHORITY

The fundamental process of revolution is that of the breakdown of previous systems of authority and government, and the construction of new systems of authority on a new basis. Consequently, it would be surprising if either of these books were not organized in the first instance around a theory of authority. For de Tocqueville, who in this book was analyzing the Old Regime for the decay of authority, the crucial question was the legitimacy of taxes, tithes, and rents—those devices by which the authority of government is used to extract wealth from the productive population either for its own functions and benefit, or for the functions and benefit of the church and the landowing classes. And as far as the book has a core argument, it is

> The French nobility has stubbornly held aloof from the other classes and had succeeded in getting themselves exempted from most of their duties to the community, fondly imagining they could keep their lofty status while evading its obligations. At first it seemed they had succeeded, but soon a curious internal malady attacked them, whose effect was, so to speak, to make them gradually crumple up, though no external pressure of any kind was brought to bear. The more their immunities increased, the poorer they became....In reality, however, they led nobody; they were alone, and when an attack was launched on them, their sole recourse was flight [ORR, pp. 135–136].

And although in the following passage the causal force in the explanation is concealed in the literary word *bankruptcy*, Trotsky also poses the question of revolution as that of the ideological basis of authority:

> But it would be the crudest mistake to assume that the second revolution [October, the one that brought the Bolsheviks to power] was accomplished eight months after the first owing to the fact that the bread ration was lowered during that period from one-and-a-half to three-quarters of a pound.... Nevertheless the hopes of the counter-revolutionary politicians for a new overturn were defeated every time. This circumstance can only seem puzzling only to one who looks upon the insurrection of the masses as "spontaneous"—that is, as a herd mutiny artificially made use of by leaders. In reality the mere existence of privations is not enough to cause an insurrection; if it were, the masses would be always in revolt. It is necessary that the bankruptcy of the social regime, being conclusively revealed, should make

these privations intolerable, and that new conditions and new ideas should open the prospect of a revolutionary way out. Then in the cause of the great aims conceived by them, those same masses will prove capable of enduring doubled and tripled privations [HRR, II, p. vii].

As we have seen previously, in the passage about "social weight," Trotsky, like de Tocqueville, is entirely aware that the previous success-ful preservation of legal privileges does not, in time of revolution, pre-serve a social position. And like Trotsky, de Tocqueville rejects the ex-planation of revolution in terms of deprivations in very nearly the same language.

Patiently endured so long as it seemed beyond redress, a grievance comes to appear intolerable once the possibility of removing it crosses men's minds. For the mere fact that certain abuses have been remedied draws attention to the others and they now appear more galling; people may suffer less, but their sensibility is exacerbated. At the height of its power feudalism did not inspire so much hatred as it did on the eve of its eclipse [ORR, p. 177].

What then is the content of Trotsky's "bankruptcy" or the final failure of de Tocqueville's "patient endurance" which sustained the Old Regime?

### AUTHORITY AND EFFECTIVENESS

De Tocqueville summarizes the feudal (i.e., pre-eighteenth century) regime of the nobles as follows:

The nobility was regarded in the age of feudalism much as the government is regarded by everyone today; its exactions were tolerated in view of the protec-tion and security it provided. True, the nobles enjoyed invidious privileges and rights that weighed heavily on the commoner, but in return for this they kept order, administered justice, saw to the execution of the laws, came to the rescue of the oppressed, and watched over the interests of all. The more these functions passed out of the hands of the nobility, the more uncalled-for did their privileges appear—until at last their mere existence seemed a meaning-less anachronism [ORR, p. 30].

And a quotation summarizing for de Tocqueville what he thought was the central difficulty of the clergy, quoted from a *cahier* of the nobles: "Tithes are for the most part exacted by those curés who give them-selves the least trouble to supply their flock with spiritual food [ORR, p. 268]."

The basic notion in both these passages is that effectiveness, especially in services to the public, legitimates authority, and ineffectiveness makes the privileges of authority galling.

Trotsky, in diagnosing during the Revolution (he is here quoting what he wrote at the time) the failure of government authority in the army, uses much the same logic:

> The organization of supplies for the army reflects the general economic collapse, against which a government constituted like the present one cannot take a single radical measure....The government... has exposed before the army... its incapacity to determine Russia's policy independently of the will of the imperialist Allies. No result is possible but the progressive breakdown of the army....The mass desertions... are ceasing in the present conditions to be the result of depraved individual wills, and are becoming an expression of the complete incapacity of the government to weld the revolutionary army with an inward unity of purposes. [The government could not make up its mind] to an immediate annulment of landlordship—that is, to the sole measure which would convince the most backward peasant that this revolution is his revolution....In such material and spiritual conditions an offensive must inevitably have the character of an adventure [HRR, I, p. 382].

And earlier, concerning the reason that the Revolution will weather the ordeal of hunger while "at present what troubles is not hunger but doubt, indefiniteness, uncertainty of tomorrow," he says:

> But while approaching these problems economically, the Compromisers [the Social Revolutionaries and the Mensheviks of the Provisional Government] made the solution of them impossible politically. Every economic problem they encountered turned into a condemnation of the dual power; every decision they had to sign burned their fingers unbearably [HRR, I, p. 239].

Since Trotsky's main problem was to explain not why the tsar fell but why the Kerensky government fell, he concentrates on the causes of the incapacity of that government. We have noticed some of this above in characterizing Kerensky's party, the Social Revolutionaries. But Trotsky traces this incapacity back to the social conformation of Russia. It is not merely the way history happened to come out that the compromise regime could not do anything. The basic cause was that the bourgeoisie could not do anything revolutionary because of their fear of the proletariat and peasantry. And the compromisers, by having to have someone to compromise with, were required to compromise with a social group that wanted to do nothing about any of the compromiser's own socialist ideals, the basis on which the masses had trusted them.

The incapacity of the bourgeoisie for political action was immediately caused by its relation to the proletariat and the peasantry. It could not lead after it workers who stood hostile in their everyday life, and had so early learned to generalize their problems. But it was likewise incapable of leading after it the peasantry, because it was entangled in a web of interests with the landlords, and dreaded the shakeup of property relations in any form [HRR].

And it is this structually induced incapacity to take any relevant political action that was at the core of the ironic treatment Trotsky gives the compromise leaders. In explaining why his irony is different from "that purely individualistic irony which spreads out like a smoke of indifference over the whole effort and intention of mankind," he says:

> The heroine of Dickens who tried to hold back the tide with a broom is an acknowledged comic image because of the fatal lack of correspondence between means and end....Tseretelli, the actual inspiritor of the dual-power regime, confessed... "Everything we did at that time was a vain effort to hold back a destructive elemental flood with a handful of insignificant chips."... To renounce irony in depicting "revolutionists" who tried to hold back a revolution with chips, would be to plunder reality and betray objectivism for the benefit of pedants [HRR, II, pp. viii–ix].

Even though Trotsky explains that many of the oppressed nationalities of Russia opposed the Soviet regime during the civil war, he points out how the incapacity of the February regime to do anything about the nationalities problem sapped their authority.

> This inevitable national disguise of social contradictions—less developed in the borderlands anyway, as a general rule—adequately explains why the October revolution was destined to meet more opposition in most of the oppressed nations than in Central Russia. But on the other hand, the conflict of nationalities by its very nature cruelly shook the February régime and created sufficiently favorable surroundings for the revolution in the center [HRR, III, p. 49].

As we might expect if authority depends on doing something, both de Tocqueville and Trotsky argue that sheer inefficiency can undermine authority. Talking of the results of venality of office, de Tocqueville writes that

> In the result, the administrative machinery which was thus built up year by year became so intricate and inefficient that it had to be left running idle, so to speak, while alongside it was set up another instrument of government, at once simpler and easier to manipulate, which in practice carried out the

functions nominally performed by the horde of office holders who had bought their way into the bureaucracy. It is obvious that no one of these pernicious institutions would have survived for long had free discussion of them been permitted. [And he quotes a comment on the problem by the Estates General of the fifteenth century] "the right of battening on the people's flesh and blood without discussion by the Three Estates and without their consent" [ORR, p. 105].

Trotsky speaks of Tsar Nicholas' choice of higher civil servants: "He selected his ministers on a principle of continual deterioration. Men of brain and character he summoned only in extreme situations when there was no other way out [HRR, I, pp. 55–56]"; or of the women who flocked to the municipal duma (a traditional government council), demanding bread: "It was like demanding milk from a he-goat [HRR, I, p. 102]." These are not, of course, for all their magnificent contemptuousness, mere literary devices, for they are offered in the context of explaining why the regime of which they were constituents failed to hold power.


## THE SOCIAL CONSTRUCTION
## OF AUTHORITATIVE PURPOSES

The conviction by the population that the achievement of social purposes depends on the authority and power of a given state apparatus is, then, at the core of the sociology of authority of both de Tocqueville and Trotsky. But clearly the distribution among the social organs of the faith of various groups in the population is a fluctuating matter, especially during the revolution itself. This is in many ways the central dependent variable of both analyses, how the social patterns of the society, the practices of government, and social events, cause different distributions of faith in the purposes of authorities and in their effectiveness, as compared with the effectiveness of their alternatives.

But perhaps the crucial determinant of the outcome in the process of judgment of purpose and effectiveness is what a social organ is compared with. In fact, the very first question is whether the existing organs are inevitable or not. If the world is inevitable, as Leibnitz first, then Dr. Pangloss, observed, it is the best of all possible worlds. In discussing the interwar years (between 1905 and 1914), Trotsky makes the following comment:

Factories which two or three years ago would strike unanimously over some single arbitrary police action, today have completely lost their revolutionary color, and accept the most monstrous crimes of the authorities without resistance. Great defeats discourage people for a long time. The consciously revolutionary elements lose their power over the masses. Prejudices and superstitions not yet burnt out come back to life. Gray immigrants from the village during these times dilute the workers' ranks. Sceptics ironically shake their heads. So it was in the years 1907–1911. But molecular processes in the masses are healing the psychological wounds of defeat. A new turn of events, or an underlying economic impulse, opens a new political cycle. The revolutionary elements again find their audience [*HRR*, I, pp. 35–36].

The significance of a defeat is not only, of course, that it punished people for revolt and sent the leadership to Siberia or Switzerland or New York; it is also that it extinguished the sense of possibility, that alternative possibility against which the constituted authorities looked bad. Trotsky comments on the same process of opening up possibilities among the peasantry in the army. "It is only in the artificial conditions of the front or in the city barrack that the young peasants, overcoming to a certain degree their isolation, would come face-to-face with problems of nation-wide scope [*HRR*, III, p. 20]." This opening of the possibilities then leads directly to Trotsky's response to a newspaper account which says, "Cultural work in the county is accompanied with a certain risk, unless one categorically promises to cooperate toward the immediate transfer of all the land to the peasants." Trotsky comments: "Where agreement and even intercourse between the fundamental classes of the population becomes impossible, the ground for democratic institutions disappears." So that, as a commissar says, "The local peasantry have got the fixed opinion that all civil laws have lost their force, and that all legal relations ought now to be regulated by peasant organizations [*HRR*, III, p. 29]." But this developing sense of possibilities then renders to other organs which pursue purposes in a trustworthy way a growing authority:

> The head land committee, consisting of governmental functionaries, landlords, professors, scientific agriculturists, Social Revolutionary politicians, and an admixture of dubious peasants, became in essence the main brake of the agrarian revolution....The town committees, however—elected by the peasants and working right there before the eyes of the village—became the instruments of the agrarian movement. The circumstance that the members of these committees usually registered as Social Revolutionaries made no difference. They kept step with the peasant's hut and not the lord's manor. The peasants especially treasured the state character of their land committees, seeing in this a sort of patent-right to civil war. [Then follows a list of quotations about how peasants will pay no attention to anyone but town committees; *HRR*, III, p. 27].

Given this dependence of authority on predictions of the future, both de Tocqueville and Trotsky emphasize how uncertainty undermines authority. Tocqueville, for example, waxes eloquent about how the perfidy of the Royal Exchequer rendered all property rights insecure.

> In records of the period we constantly read of royal property being sold, then declared "unsaleable" and taken back; of broken pledges; of established rights being brushed aside. . . .Privileges granted in perpetuity were constantly withdrawn. Indeed, if mishaps to a foolish vanity deserved any pity we could hardly help sympathizing with these unlucky people who, after having acquired a patent of nobility, were forced time and again during the seventeenth and eighteenth centuries to repurchase the unjust privileges. . . ."Call the titles having been obtained by surprise" as the edict quaintly phrases it [ORR, p. 101].

Or Trotsky explaining succinctly why the decisions of the state Dumas were not being executed: "Everyone felt that the last word had not yet been spoken [HRR, I, p. 47]." Conversely, of course, uncertainty of the Revolution undermines *its* authority:

> The more the soldiers in their mass are convinced that the rebels are really rebelling—that this is not a demonstration after which they will have to go back to the barracks and report, that this is a struggle to the death, that the people may win if they join them, and that this winning will not only guarantee impunity, but allieviate the lot of all—the more they realize this, the more willing they are to turn aside their bayonets [HRR, I, p. 121].

And Tocqueville, though more interested in how to prevent people imagining that they can quickly and easily make society better, undertakes to explain the extraordinary role of intellectuals in convincing people that "simple elementary rules deriving from the exercise of the human reason and natural law" could drastically improve the lot of man:

> If the French people had still played an active part in politics [through the Estates General] or even if they had merely continued to concern themselves with the day-to-day administration of affairs through the provincial assemblies, we may be sure that they would not have let themselves be carried away so easily by the ideas of the writers of the day; any experience, however slight, of public affairs would have made them chary of accepting the opinion of mere theoreticians [ORR, p. 141].

And Trotsky, conversely, argues that without gradually building up in the masses a conviction that they can indeed, as a practical matter, run a revolution, their conviction that the Revolution itself is more than a mere theoretical matter without authority, also cannot form:

> A revolutionary uprising that spreads over a number of days can develop victoriously only in case it ascends step by step, and scores one success after another. A pause in its growth is dangerous: a prolonged marking of time, fatal....But for this very reason [of several days of success] the movement had arrived at a level where mere symptomatic successes were not enough [*HRR*, I, p. 110].

Now what ties these various considerations together? They are all directed at the problem of explaining the decay of authority, they all have something to do with people forming purposes and believing, or not believing, that particular social organs are effective in pursuing those purposes, and they have to do with the perception of possibilities. Let us try to construct the abstract model of man that is involved in these explanations, so as to see what is going on in them.

First, it is clear to both Trotsky and de Tocqueville that people do not have real attitudes toward authorities regarded as inevitable, attitudes in the sense of an independent judgment that can play a causal role in the fate of the institution. An institution has authority when it is regarded as inevitable: *Insofar* as one is going to pursue the purposes pursued by the institution, one is going to pursue them through that institution. Thus if the institution is ineffective, the authority it holds may not be very enthusiastically believed in; it may be fragile in the face of a revolutionary process that throws up alternative possibilities, but it is not subject to challenge so long as it is inevitable. This inevitability is why military and political defeats take so long to cure, and why the uncertain masses do not trust themselves to make a revolution, why the soldiers imagine that they will have to go back to the barracks to face the consequences for joining the masses. It is also why the conviction of the possibility of reform, inculcated by the Enlightenment thinkers, seemed so important to de Tocqueville, for it made the Old Regime no longer inevitable (in fact made it seem very easy to make it very much better by the application of simple dictates of human reason). The gradual spreading of the conviction that perhaps a better alternative is really possible, that perhaps through, for example, the land committees, the land can really be divided up again, is what both Trotsky and de Tocqueville see as the basic psychological process of undermining the traditional authority. And the embedding of that alternative in revolutionary institutions, so that people pursue their purposes through them rather than through the Old Regime, is what the regime of "dual power", which we shall analyze shortly, is all about.

The fickleness of the masses during a revolution thus takes on a completely different interpretation. Trotsky's sarcasm about spontaneity as an explanation of the movements is essentially an assertion that the explanations of the masses about why they are doing what they are doing are going to be reasonable, but that reasonableness is going to be based on their estimates of the probabilities that (*a*) this institution or authority will pursue my goals; or (*b*) this institution or authority is the best I am likely to find, because no alternatives are possible or because the alternatives are in the hands of the enemy. And it is these probabilities that fluctuate wildly during a revolution but are reasonably stable during times of governmental quiescence. But the alternatives, and the probabilities about the future, are imaginative constructions— solidly institutionalized imagination during times of social peace, subject to the influence of events as the future is reconstructed daily by the fates of various revolutionary and traditional authorities during time of revolution.

## DEMOCRACY, LIBERTY, AND AUTHORITY

If this argument is true, then the common belief of de Tocqueville and Trotsky that democratic discussion is good for the stability of authority should be related to it. One part of the argument of de Tocqueville was implicit in the passage quoted earlier in which he argues that reasonable expectations of public policy tend to be encouraged by participation in the making of public policy. But the other part of his argument is summarized in the following passage:

> Political freedom is no less indispensable to the ruling classes to enable them to realize their perils than to the rank and file to enable them to safeguard their rights. . . .The small disturbances which, when there is political freedom, inevitably take place from time to time in even the most stable social systems are a constant reminder of the risk of large scale cataclysms and keep the authorities on the *qui vive*. But. . . on the very eve of the revolution, there had been as yet no warning that the ancient edifice was tottering [*ORR*, p. 143].

Trotsky does not, of course, believe that the tsar, or the bourgeois republic, could have introduced democracy and political freedom in Russia without bringing the whole system of property relations crashing down, and so losing the support of the nobility and the bourgeoisie themselves. But he is very much concerned with the capacity of the Bolshevik party to correct its mistakes, to keep in tune with the masses so that its authority will be accepted.

> If all the conferences, debates, personal quarrels which took place in the upper layer of the Bolshevik party during October alone had been taken down by a stenographer, posterity might convince itself with what intense inner struggle the determination necessary for the overthrow was crystallized among the heads of the party. The stenographic report would show at the same time how much a revolutionary party has need of internal democracy. The will to struggle is not stored up in advance, and is not dictated from above—it has on every occasion to be independently renewed and tempered. ...The high temper of the Bolshevik party expressed itself not in an absence of disagreements, waverings, and even quakings, but in the fact that in the most difficult circumstances it gathered itself in good season by means of inner crises [HRR, III, pp. 165–166].

The same argument of democracy aiding authority was implicit in the passage quoted earlier in which Trotsky is explaining why the peasantry tended to trust the town committees of agricultural affairs but not the higher bodies.

### AUTHORITY AND INEQUALITY OR "JUSTICE"

De Tocqueville had a much more specific theory of what it was about inequality in the Old Regime that undermined authority than Trotsky had. The reasons for this is two fold. First, Trotsky regarded the injustices of capitalism and feudalism as inevitable parts of their social order, not as something requiring special explanation. Perhaps the intensity of class antagonism, greater in Russia than in the rest of Europe, required explanation in terms of the penetration of advanced capitalist stratification intensifying and combining with "feudal" forms in the peripheral countries (HRR, I, pp. 3–15), but the evils of capitalism and of feudalism are inherent in them and need neither be explained nor (except in a general way of blaming the whole system) blamed. For de Tocqueville, however, who wants to figure out how to make feudalism work, the features which excite indignation in feudal regimes demand explanation and require blame to those who undermined the feudal regime. Second, de Tocqueville regarded the fundamental stratification relation of the Old Regime to be governmental rather than feudal. This meant that the principal stratification relations of the Old Regime were matters of government policy rather than a part of society outside the government.

This last is a crucial point on which de Tocqueville is often misunderstood. De Tocqueville did not (except inadvertently—and unfortunately, he is not always consistent here) "substitute" a governmental theory of the revolution for a class theory. Instead, he started off with the observation that, besides governmentally guaranteed property rights of various kinds, the government itself not only distributed a large part of the national income of France directly but also distributed both capital goods and the legal property rights previously mentioned and apportioned the taxation and expropriation to carry this tremendous burden. Thus there were *two* fundamental class relations in the Old Regime, landlord versus peasant *and* tax collector versus peasant (and of course corresponding to this latter, the relation of tax collector and beneficiary of government grants). It was at least as much this stratification by government policy that came under attack in the revolution as the stratification by landed property. While Trotsky takes the Tsarist regime to be the creature of the nobility, de Tocqueville's principal argument is that the nobility had become the creature of the state bureaucracy. This means that de Tocqueville has, so to speak, voluntary government actions creating injustices to analyze. If property is theft, Trotsky assumes that the theft is of ancient vintage, de Tocqueville that it is still going on and ought to be stopped, so that "established rights" can be protected (see the previous quotation about broken government pledges).

> Of all the various ways of making men conscious of their differences and of stressing class distinctions, unequal taxation is the most pernicious, since it creates a permanent estrangement between those who benefit and those who suffer by it. Once the principle is established that noblemen and commoners are not to be taxed at the same rates, the public is reminded of the distinction drawn between them year by year when the imposts are assessed and levied. Thus on these occasions each member of the privileged class takes notice of the practical interest he has in differentiating himself from the masses and in stiffening the barriers between himself and them. Since so many debates on public affairs concern an existing tax or the imposition of a new one, it is obvious that when one section of the community is exempt and another subject to it, they will rarely see eye to eye or wish to meet together to exchange ideas [*ORR*, p. 92].

Of course the matter is not as clear as this passage makes it, since, as de Tocqueville acknowledges (*ORR*, p. 92), there were more bourgeois exempted from taxation than nobles, and it was quite easy for a commoner to become a noble ("In no other period of French history was it so easy to acquire a title as in 1789 [*ORR*, p. 89]").

In fact, this is one of the places in which de Tocqueville's tendency to contradict himself is so strong that it is hard to know when one is representing his argument rightly. The problem is that he has to explain why France had a revolution and England did not, a circumstance that he hopes to attribute to the different characters of their nobilities. In the first place, there is at least one king of England who might be glad to be here to dispute with de Tocqueville about whether England had a revolution, and at least one provincial rebellion centered in Massachusetts and Virginia that had some borrowings from the Enlightenment. In the second place, de Tocqueville uses the participation of the public in forming public policy together with the nobility to explain why England had no revolution (pp. 97–98) and why France had one (p. 200); the nobility's subjection to greater taxes in England to explain the lack of revolution (p. 98) while the tendency of the royal treasury to milk the privileged classes in France explains the revolution (p. 101); the castelike character of the French nobility and its greater tendency to set itself off with barriers is offered to explain revolution, while we just saw that the nobility was perhaps more open in France to new recruitment and that nobility of office was very widespread, and many noble privileges were available with venal offices even when these were not formally noble offices. The superior openness of England is not established. These same tendencies to idealize successful feudal regimes also show up in inaccuracies about medieval France (even aside from de Tocqueville's quaint notion that freedom is increased by serfdom). I propose that we ignore de Tocqueville's historical method whenever its purpose is to present a praiseworthy feudal regime to contrast with the bad Old Regime.

Further, de Tocqueville argues that it was an increase in this yearly reminder of injustice that cut classes off from each other more and more:

> The *taille* . . . had risen tenfold and all new taxes were assimilated to it [this is false; most new revenue came from increased returns from taxes on commerce, the General Farms, A.L.S.]. Thus year by year the inequality of taxation created an ever wider rift between classes, dividing up the nation more and more into watertight compartments. Once taxation had been so contrived as to press most heavily on those who had least means of defending themselves against it, and not on those most capable of bearing the burden, the result was as inevitable as it was detested: the rich got off scot free and the poor suffered accordingly [*ORR*, p. 100].

What de Tocqueville is trying to explain here is *effortful distinctions*, that is, people *pursuing the intention* of distinguishing themselves socially and in legal privileges from other people. His argument is that the more people are induced to do this, the less, in other words, their privileges grow naturally out of the interactions and property relations, the more illegitimate they will seem. Thus he is particularly attentive to purely honorary distinctions, and says, "Generally speaking, the nobility, while abandoning many of their beneficial rights, cling with anxiety and warmth to those which are purely honorary [*ORR*, p. 267]." Clearly de Tocqueville must be up to something that he thinks theoretically important, because in making this statement he contradicts evidence he himself offers only a couple of pages later:

> In any event, the nobility demand that each Order preserve the dignity that is meet in Frenchmen; that consequently, the old humiliating forms which were imposed on the Third Estate—such as bending the knee—be abolished. One *cahier* says that the "sight of one man on his knees before another is offensive to the dignity of man [*ORR*, p. 269].

What can de Tocqueville be trying to do in this whole analysis of the relation between authority and privileges, which he regards as important enough to get himself into contradictions?

It seems to me that he is trying to construct the system of legally guaranteed privileges out of their constituent human actions, which are shaped by motives, on the one hand, and constraints of the individual's situation, on the other. These actions are, on the one hand, the individual claim of a privilege and an individual grant by the government or recognition in a court of that privilege and, on the other hand, a political defense of the classification of people in the society by the criteria that are used to define privileged classes. The argument that would be consistent with his previous argument about authority would be that *if* the principles by which privileges are distributed are publicly debated up to the point where they are consented to by some large minority of the leading population, and *if* then the grants of individual privilege are allocated on that ground, rather than arbitrarily by the will of the king, *then* most men, most of the time, when confronted by the unpleasant fact that others have more privileges than they, will have the unpleasantness moderated by general public consent to the system of privilege and by the confidence that the particular privilege was deserved by that standard.

De Tocqueville went wrong in not following his argument consistently, in trying to substitute easy structural contrasts between open and closed aristocracies, or participant versus nonparticipant constitutions

in local government, or selfish French upper classes compared to generous British ones. But these structural concepts are not built up carefully
out of the intentions and possibilities of individuals as these are socially
patterned, and consequently they require him either to give up his argument or to contradict his own assessment of the facts. It is testimony
to de Tocqueville's seriousness as a historian that he would rather contradict himself than not report the facts as he sees them. But it is not
much help in our extraction of the grounds upon which rest his bril-
liance as a theorist.

## STRUCTURES OF AUTHORITY AND STRATEGIC GROUPS

We are now in a better position to understand the crucial causal importance that both analysts give to certain strategic groups, particularly
to the army and the nobility. Trotsky states the crucial importance of the
army quite bluntly:

> The right to control bodies of armed men is a fundamental right of the state
> power. The first Provisional Government, wished upon the people by the
> Executive Committee [of the Soviet], gave an obligation not to disarm and not
> to remove from Petrograd those military units which had taken part in the
> February overturn. This was the formal beginning of a military dualism insep-
> arable in essence from the double sovereignty [HRR, III, p. 88].

Or this:

> Against a numerous, disciplined, well-armed and ably led military force, un-
> armed or almost unarmed masses of the people cannot possibly gain a victory
> [HRR, I, p. 120].

And he locates the crucial turning points of the Revolution by the reaction of military units. A meeting of a crowd of workers with the Cos-
sacks in February 1917:

> Cutting their way with the breasts of their horses, the officers first charged
> through the crowd. Behind them, filling the whole width of the Prospect,
> galloped the Cossacks. Decisive moment! But the horsemen, cautiously, in a
> long ribbon, rode through the corridor just made by the officers. "Some of
> them smiled," Kayurov recalls, "and one of them gave the workers a good
> wink.". . . Of discipline there remained but a thin transparent shell that
> threatened to break through any second. . . .All these things, however, were
> merely significant symptoms. The army was still the army, it was bound with

discipline, and the threads were in the hands of the monarchy [*HRR*, I, pp. 104–105].

But what is perhaps more surprising is the importance Trotsky attributes to the nobility in the revolution:

> Russia proved again, both in 1905 and yet more in 1917, that a revolution directed against an autocratic and half feudal régime, and consequently against a nobility, meets in its first step an unsystematic and inconsistent but nevertheless very real coöperation not only from the rank and file nobility, but also from its most privileged upper circles. . . .The privileged caste cannot believe that no policy whatever is possible which would reconcile the old society with the new. . . .The sharpness and irresponsibility of the aristocratic opposition is explained by history's having made spoiled children of the upper circles of the nobility. . . .The unsystematic and inconsistent character of the noble discontent is explained by the fact that it is the opposition of a class which has no future . . . the nobility before disappearing gives out an oppositional flash, which performs a mighty service for its mortal enemy [*HRR*, I, pp. 76–77].

And de Tocqueville, not so concerned with the mechanics of the Revolution and thus less interested in the army, spends several pages of his notes on the contribution of the nobility to the origin of the Revolution, summarizing it as follows:

> Like all other Frenchmen, [the nobility] regard France as a trial field—a sort of political model farm—in which everything should be tried, everything turned upside down, except the little spot in which their particular privileges grow. To their honor, it may even be said that they did not wholly spare that spot. In a word, it is seen from these *cahiers* that the only thing the nobles lacked to effect the Revolution was the rank of commoners [*ORR*, pp. 262–272, the quoted summary appearing on 272].

In both cases, these strategic groups play the role of opening up or cutting off the sense of possibilities for the revolutionaries. The inevitability of being driven off with Cossack whips or bullets changes to the possibility of demonstrating and still staying alive; the inevitability that the monarchy, joined by the nobility, always wins against reform efforts changes to the possibility of reform with support in high places. That is, these groups play during time of revolution much the same role that Trotsky attributes to the legality of the peasant town committees, in the passage already quoted—or the great influence de Tocqueville attributes to the provincial assemblies that were "invested with most of the powers that had hitherto been the Intendants' [*ORR*, p. 196]" so that "no one knew from whom he should take orders, to whom he should apply, or how to solve those small private problems which crop up almost daily in the life of every member of a social group [*ORR*, p. 203]" that opened up the possibility of doing anything that might occur to someone in the last days of the Old Regime.

## AUTHORITY AND SYMBOLS

Symbols occur all through the passages quoted thus far, ranging from the wink of the Cossack, the patent of nobility, to the "patent right to civil war." But these symbols occur in the course of daily action and seem to have little to do with those symbol systems of religion or the divine right of kings or national patriotism and German gold that are supposed to be so important to legitimacy. Trotsky in fact takes the issue directly in hand with a statement that amounts to the assertion that such general symbols occur in political discourse only when people have difficulty relating what they want to what they can practically do:

> Their industrial isolation makes the peasants, so determined in struggle with a concrete landlord, impotent before the general landlord incarnate in the state. Hence the organic need of the muzhiks to rely upon some legendary state as against the real one. In olden times they created pretenders, they united round an imagined Golden Edict of the Tsar, or around the legend of a righteous world. After the February revolution they united round the Social Revolutionary banner "Land and Freedom," seeking help in it against the liberal landlord who had become a governmental commissar. The Narodnik program [i.e., "Land and Freedom"] bore the same relation to the real government of Kerensky, as the imagined edict of the tsar to the real autocrat [*HRR*, III, p. 18].

And de Tocqueville, contemptuous as he is of "men who seek to compensate for their grovelling servility to the meanest jack-in-office by declaiming against God," doubts the crucial character of the antireligious ideology of the Revolution in unequivocal terms:

> It is easy enough to see today that the campaign against all forms of religion was merely incidental to the French Revolution, a spectacular but transient phenomenon, a brief reaction to the ideologies, emotions, and events which led up to it—but in no sense basic to its program [*ORR*, p. 6].

What makes symbols relevant to authority is their capacity to *commit* authority, that is, to make everyone believe that what is *going* to happen is what *has* to happen, that it is purposive and compares well with all alternatives that are thinkable, if any are, so that the possibility of resistance seems fruitless. Vague general legitimations do not do this, because there are always people close enough to the actions of authorities to see alternatives, and if they are interested and can build up public support, capable of leading the first part of the revolution. Trotsky points to this clearly when he is explaining (perhaps in refutation of de Tocqueville) why the revolution is concentrated in the capital city:

> It is often said, especially in regard to the great French revolution, that the extreme centralization of the monarchy subsequently permits the revolutionary capital to think and act for the whole country. That explanation is superficial. . . . The provinces accept the steps taken by the capital as their own intentions already materialized. . . . The rôle of the capital is determined not by the tradition of a bureaucratic centralism, but by the situation of the leading revolutionary class, whose vanguard is naturally concentrated in the chief city: this is equally true for the bourgeoisie and the proletariat [*HRR*, I, pp. 140–141].

But it is clear from his recurrent analysis of the vanguard party and the reason the proletariat was the vanguard class that what he means by *vanguard* is the group which perceives the possibilities in the situation and how they can be achieved: Through what mechanisms and with the support of which forces. Thus it is a virtue of the vanguard party *not* to take power in July, when they could not hold it (*HRR*, II, Chapter III is called "Could the Bolsheviks Have Seized the Power in July?"), while we saw the Party praised for seeing the possibility of taking and holding it in October.

## AUTHORITY AND DUAL POWER

Now if we turn to look at the institutional situation that de Tocqueville and Trotsky were analyzing specifically, we can see why their strategies are so similar. Both of them are analyzing a situation of dual power. This is obvious enough with Trotsky, because that is what he explicitly says in the most brilliant theoretical chapter in the book, where he defines the Revolution as the development of dual power (*HRR*, I, pp. 206–215). But it is also true of de Tocqueville. When he is explicitly describing the purpose of his study, he goes to considerable lengths to disabuse us of the notion that he is going to study why people went out into the streets in 1789.

Since the object of the Revolution was not merely to change an old form of government but to abolish the entire social structure of pre-revolutionary France, it was obliged to declare war simultaneously on all established powers, to destroy all recognized prerogatives, to make short work of all traditions, and to institute new ways of living, new conventions. Thus one of its first acts was to rid men's minds of all those notions which had ensured their obedience to authority under the old régime. Hence its so markedly anarchic tendencies. But beneath the seemingly chaotic surface there was developing a vast, highly centralized power which attracted to itself and welded into an organic whole all the elements of authority and influence that hitherto had been dispersed among a crowd of lesser, unco-ordinated powers [ORR, p. 8].

But de Tocqueville's historical work is about the prerevolutionary period, surely not the same sort of situation that Trotsky talked about. When we examine de Tocqueville's theory of what had happened to the feudal regime, it is precisely that its true sovereignty had been sapped by the growth of a dual power, the royal bureaucracy. De Tocqueville writes an appendix on the Pays of Languedoc precisely because the corrosion of feudal virtue by the growth of royal authority has not gone so far there as in the rest of France. The public functions of the nobility in the rest of France were no longer connected to their privileges because the royal bureaucracy was slowly gaining power to administer local affairs, while the noble himself perhaps moved to the city. Thus what interested de Tocqueville about the Old Regime was how authority got transferred to the royal bureaucracy and away from assemblies of privileged people, the Estates General, and so on.

Thus in both cases there is a concrete entity, either the Soviet or the king's men, who are progressively taking over authority, sapping the opposing institutions of their inner coherence, of their capacity to organize men's purposes through themselves, of their feeling of inevitability. And it is because both Trotsky and de Tocqueville were theorists of structural choices (which then have to be resolved into individual choices), of choices that varied over time and among social classes, that they are forced to develop a theory of authority deeper than the sorts of mechanical formulas with which we have unfortunately been burdened in this field, of authority being "power combined with legitimacy," or "probabilities of obtaining one's will against resistance," or other socially empty abstractions.

## THE IMPLICATIONS OF THE PRECEDING DISCUSSION

Let us suppose that the reader now accepts the outline of the theory of authority presented in this chapter as (a) correctly representing what

Trotsky and de Tocqueville thought about authority; (b) a theory which could be applied to other authorities; and (c) better than the kind of theory that tries to attach enough adjectives to power to turn it into authority. What this shows is then that there is a methodological lesson to learn; it does not show what that lesson is. Are we confronted with the hopeless fact that de Tocqueville and Trotsky were extraordinary men and thus doomed to wait for their like before we can advance further? I think not.

What I will be trying to show in the following sections of this chapter is that de Tocqueville and Trotsky both follow similar *strategies* in dealing with the facts of history, which results in their wringing from them concepts which come closer to reality and are consequently more general. These strategies will be of a very abstract character, so the ratio of my text to theirs will increase as I try to explain what I see.

## GEOGRAPHICAL, SOCIAL, OR POLITICAL DISTRIBUTION AS AN INDEX OF A PROCESS

The first strategy is easiest for a sociologist to locate because it is identical with the one he or she has been taught in elementary methodology. This is inferring the nature of the causal process from static correlations. Trotsky particularly views Russia in thoroughly statistical terms, and keeps in his interpretative armory a set of cross-sectional comparisons which give a clue to the causal process, and therefore to the future. The most frequent is the range of political parties from both ends toward the middle; Bolsheviks to Menseviks to Social Revolutionaries; and Tsarist bureaucracy and officer corps to Kadets to Social Revolutionaries. But these comparisons are supplemented with the comparisons of Vyborg district (of Petersburg) to Petersburg, Petersburg to Moscow, Moscow to provincial cities, provincial cities to the villages; proletariat to sailors to soldiers to peasants; Russia to the Slavic minorities (Ukranians and Belorussians) to the Caucasian minorities to the Turkish minorities to the Siberian minorities; Lenin to the Bolsheviks with historical imagination to the mediocrities.

At any given time the cross-sectional distribution of a given sentiment is a clue to what is coming next. When the Petersburg proletariat is discouraged and the Petersburg garrison goes from supportive to neutral, the Bolsheviks are in for retreats throughout the country. When Lenin sees something, soon the whole party will see it. When the Baltic Sea fleet is ready for insurrection, we can expect the army masses to swing over in a few days or weeks. When the army general staff and the Kadets have enough courage and solidarity to try a coup, the Social

Revolutionaries will be torn apart, with a right wing going along and a left wing nervous and impotent. When Bolshevik policies of immediate seizure of landlord property and soldiers going home become widespread in the villages, the political penetration of the society is complete except for convincing them that only the Soviets, and particularly the Bolshevik Soviets, will legitimate those policies.

That is, Trotsky carries around a social map of Russia, and what an event portends depends on its place in that map. The map itself is carefully constructed by the differences in causal processes that interest him. For instance, consider this establishment of the difference between the situation of the worker and that of the soldier in Petrograd, a comparison used over and over again throughout the book in assessing what a given actions means:

> The army is heterogeneous, and its antagonistic elements are held together by the terror of discipline. On the very eve of the decisive hour, the revolutionary soldiers do not know how much power they have, or what influence they can exert. The working masses, of course, are also heterogeneous. But they have immeasurably more opportunity for testing their ranks in the process of preparation for the decisive encounter. Strikes, meetings, demonstrations, are not only acts in the struggle, but also measures of its force. The whole mass does not participate in the strike. Not all the strikers are ready to fight. In the sharpest moments the most daring appear in the streets. The hesitant, the tired, the conservative, sit at home. Here a revolutionary selection takes place of itself; people are sifted through the sieve of events. It is otherwise with the army. The revolutionary soldiers—sympathetic, wavering or antagonistic—all are tied together by a compulsory discipline whose threads are held, up to the last moment, in the officer's fist. The soldiers are told off daily into first and second files, but how are they to be divided into rebellious and obedient? The psychological moment when the soldiers go over to the revolution is prepared by a long molecular process, which like other processes of nature, has its point of climax. . . . After [a] ripened but unrealized mutiny, a reaction may seize the army. The soldiers lose the hope which flared in their breasts, they bend their necks again to the yoke of discipline and in a new encounter with the workers, especially at a distance, will stand opposed to the insurrection [HRR, I, pp. 120–121].

Aside from the Hegelian literary figures about molecular processes reaching their climax, what is going on in this passage? A concrete comparison is being built up, that between the Petersburg garrison and the Petersburg proletariat, almost always the Vyborg district. The comparison of structures is being built up by detailed, if somewhat imaginative, reconstruction of the actions that make up the structures, and especially the *long series of actions subject to differential selective pressures* that

towns or by way of the fleet and the army or within the army from the Petersburg garrison to the backward Roumanian front, are built up, more or less carefully, with that process of revolution in mind. Insofar as this is really the process of revolution, then, the static pattern at a given moment from the vanguard to the backward regiments or villages is in fact a portent of the movements to come.

De Tocqueville uses the same general strategy, though since the events he is interpreting come in the future, beyond the end of the book, the interpenetration of narrative and causal analysis is not so obvious. The same literary devices of hollow, brittle outward shells pervade de Tocqueville's work:

> Nothing has been left that could obstruct the central government, but, by the same token, nothing could shore it up. This is why the grandiose edifice built up by our kings was doomed to collapse like a card castle once disturbances arose within the social order on which it was based [ORR, p. 137].

In another passage:

> That it was possible to build up modern institutions of this kind in France within the shattered framework of the feudal system may seem surprising at first sight. It was a task calling for much patience and adroitness rather than for the exercise of force and authoritarian methods. When the Revolution broke out, very little of the old [feudal] administrative structure had actually been destroyed; but a new substructure, so to speak, had gradually been pieced together [ORR, pp. 57–58].

The commercialization of land tenure, with the corresponding decay of the governmental and administrative significance of feudal social relations, is one variable for which Tocqueville notes the geographic distribution and the corresponding distribution of support of the Revolution (ORR, p. 25). Likewise, the participation of the nobility collectively in public administration was more preserved in the Pays d'Etat than in the Pays d'Election and more, for example, in Languedoc than in Brittany, so de Tocqueville studies Languedoc to compare it with the administration of the basins of the Seine and Loire, which were much more centrally administered. And in one extreme case:

> The Physiognomy of governments can be best detected in their colonies, for there their features are magnified, and rendered more conspicuous. When I want to discover the spirit and vices of the government of Louis XIV, I must go to Canada. Its deformities are seen there as through a microscope. A number of obstacles, created by previous occurrences or old social forms,

which hindered the development of the true tendencies of government at home, did not exist in Canada [*ORR*, p. 253].

Since the argument has to do with the growth of the dual power of the royal government as compared to the feudal regime, we see that each of the geographical comparisons is carefully constructed according to the structural distribution of those forms. To see what men pursuing the objectives of the royal government would do if they could, go to a place where they could do it, where the feudal forms had no toughness or capacity to fight back. Or conversely, to find what the nobility would do if they could, go to the lightly penetrated periphery of the country where even the absolute king had to truck and barter with the nobility to get anything done. Events and actions have different portents, depending on where they take place, for that indicates their place in the causal geography of social forms.

## THE PREDISPOSITIONS OF SYSTEMS

When de Tocqueville is describing the effects of government censorship on the conduct of writers, he says:

> And these half measures, far from weakening the power of enemies of the Church, added fuel to the fire. For if there are periods of history when the state control of writers succeeds in checking all progressive thought, there are others when it has exactly the opposite effect. But never has a policy of restrictions on the freedom of the press such as then prevailed, failed to augment [the press's] influence a hundredfold. Authors were harried to an extent that won them sympathy but not enough to inspire them with any real fear. They were, in fact, subjected to the petty persecutions that spur men to revolt, but not to the steady pressure that breaks their spirit. The legal proceedings taken against our writers were almost always dilatory, widely publicized but ineffective [*ORR*, pp. 152–153].

De Tocqueville is here talking about why the writers of the Old Regime were radical. I think he has only part of the answer, because the role of writer for a mass public who is supported to a large extent by book sales was a new one whose norms were just being worked out, and such ambiguous roles very often produce both radicalism in their holders and irritation in their role partners. But here we are interested in the structure of de Tocqueville's argument more than in the structure of society. He explains the radicalism of writers by the social organization of the system that deals with them. The outputs of the system are erratic actions because of the nature of the system. To tie this point down, let us quote Trotsky to the same effect, before analyzing what the nature of this systemic predisposition is.

> Compromisism in a time of revolution is a policy of feverish scurrying back and forth between classes. Kerensky was the incarnation of scurrying back and forth. Placed at the head of an army, an institution unthinkable without a clear and concise régime, Kerensky became the immediate instrument of its disintegration. Denekin published a curious list of changes of personnel in the high commanding staff—changes which missed the mark, although nobody really knew, and least of all Kerensky, where the mark was. Alexeiev dismissed the commander-in-chief at the front, Ruszky, and the army commander, Radko-Dmitriev, for weakness and indulgence into the committees. Brussilov removed for the same reason the panic-stricken Yudenich. Kerensky dismissed Alexeiev himself and the commanders-in-chief at the front, Gurko and Dragomirov, for resisting democratization of the army. On the same grounds Brussilov removed General Kaledin, and was himself subsequently relieved for excessive indulgence to the committees. Kornilov left the command of the Petrograd district through inability to get along with the democracy. This did not prevent his appointment to the front, and subsequently to the supreme command. Denikin was removed from the post of chief of staff under Alexeiev for his obviously feudal administration, but was soon after named commander-in-chief of the western front. This game of leap-frog, showing that the people at the top did not know what they wanted, gradually extending downward to the companies, hastened the breakdown of the army [HRR, I, p. 376].

Again we find a social system with the *disposition* to erratic behavior, and because the system produces such erratic behavior systematically, it produces in the objects of the system's policy a rebellious disposition. These systems, in their turn, produce part of the larger pattern of events which is to be interpreted, the radicalization of the intellectuals and the decline of officers' authority, respectively. But what is needed in order to proceed is a *causal characterization* of the institution. It is these rapid summaries of that part of the causal system on which the author does not want to concentrate at the moment that gives the impression of density to the analysis. On the other hand, because these causes are unanalyzed, their construction is crucial to the correctness of the whole argument.

Some of these causal characterizations have previously been developed from an explanatory scheme. For example, the character of the social base of the Social Revolutionary party, and how it differed from that of the Bolsheviks and the Kadets is part of the explanation why the leader of that party, Kerensky, and a government dominated by that party, the Provisional Government, could not follow a consistent policy. The larger explanation that Trotsky gives is that their solution to the problem of what policy to follow, namely to prosecute the war with the old generals, was not a viable policy. The generals would rather conduct a counterrevolution than prosecute the war, and soldiers would rather go home (alive) and claim their share of the landlord's land than prosecute the war. Favoring democracy in the army thus contradicted prosecuting the war. Favoring the officer corps and military discipline contradicted opposition to the counterrevolution and the favoring of parliamentary democracy in the nation. Given that Kerensky wanted a combination of impossible things, he could not follow a policy of obtaining one of them without generating the conditions under which he had to do the opposite.

De Tocqueville's causal characterization of the censorship apparatus is not so deeply embedded in his argument and may conceivably be merely a derivative of the deep belief among French intellectuals that firmness in authorities produces conformity in followers (the American prejudice is exactly the opposite, that firmness is bound to be arbitrary and to produce rebellion), and that firmness is a quality of character, a quality of being a leader. But more likely it is the result of a buried historical analysis, involving the ambivalence of the royal bureaucracy and court circles toward reason; the use by the *Parlements* or high courts of religious and other intellectual controversies as an occasion for disputing jurisdiction with the king; the beginning of the formation of noble and bureaucratic public opinion in Paris by conversations in the salons, in which the Enlightenment writers participated as well; and perhaps the concrete history of the publication of the *Encyclopedie* which was on, then off, then on again, then on again but with the printer doing his own censorship; or of Voltaire shuttling back and forth between Switzerland and France as the winds of censorship changed.

In this particular case, the problem both men are dealing with is one of social purposes not being thoroughly institutionalised, so that different parts of the apparatus, or the same part of the apparatus at different times, drift with the errant breeze. The tone of irony comes because government censorship apparatuses or armies are the sorts of social organizations that ought to have purposes, ought not to be as changeable as the moods of Kerensky, ought to be able to decide whether they want to suppress Voltaire's thoughts or not.

But we find the same general sort of quick, accurate, causal characterization for social systems that do have a purpose. For instance:

> The principles of liberalism can have a real existence only in conjunction with a police system. Anarchism is an attempt to cleanse liberalism of the

police... being a shadow-caricature of liberalism, anarchism as a whole has shared its fate....Like every sect which founds its teaching not upon the actual development of human society, but upon the reduction to absurdity of one of its features, anarchism explodes like a soap bubble at that moment when the social contradictions arrive at the points of war or revolution [*HRR*, II, pp. 179–180].

Or from de Tocqueville:

In no other European country were the ordinary courts so independent of the government as in France, but in no other country was so much use made of "exceptional" justice....Since the King could neither play on [the judges'] ambition nor inspire them with fear [there] arose the custom... of withdrawing from the ordinary courts the rights of trying cases in which the King's authority or interest was in any way involved [*ORR*, p. 52].

These two passages look as if they were directed as explaining opposite sorts of things, and in a sense they are. But there is a strong analogy in the logical nature of what they are trying to do. De Tocqueville wants to analyze why the king and the royal bureaucracy developed in such a manner that they could not justify their authority to public opinion, among other things to the *Parlements*, in various controversies just before the Revolution. That is, he wants to be able to predict a *specific incompetence* of the royal power; not being answerable to the law and to the ideas of justice institutionalized in the courts and the legal profession tended to produce that sort of incompetence. Anarchism likewise, according to Trotsky, has a specific incompetence for dealing with property relations, which—since property relations are a large part of what police and laws are about—meant that they could not deal with the *practical* problems of abolishing or redirecting the police.

These subordinate characterizations of the causal predispositions of systems are oriented around incompetences because of the role they play in the explanation of events. If an organization is the kind which will arrive at the right answer, whatever that answer is, then the problem of analyzing its behavior is simply one of deriving the right answer. Economics as a discipline is directed at giving this sort of explanation, and it shows up clearly in Trotsky's analysis of why the Bolsheviks came to the right answer about not taking power in July and taking power in October. Trotsky is cynical enough about human intelligence to believe that this rare phenomenon of a social organization with a tendency to get the right answer to difficult questions requires explanation, as we pointed out when quoting him on intraparty democracy. But intelligence, whether social or individual, is a peculiar kind of disposition to make the answer depend on the question rather than the usual kind of disposition to give a certain kind of answer. The disposition to give a certain kind of answer is a disposition to be incompetent in situations requiring another kind.

There are two principal components to these explanations of a disposition to be incompetent. The first is cognitive. The king does not see that authority answerable to the law is, in the long run, more stable than arbitrary authority. The anarchists do not see that police, at least in time of revolution, are much more intimately connected to the *interests* in social control, that is, to property interests, than the anarchist notion that governments are the source of evil can grasp.

The second part is a matter of the distribution of power resources: whether, seeing the right answer, one can do anything about it. There were some people in the Old Regime bureaucracy with both of de Tocqueville's correct solutions: freedom of publication, on the one hand, and systematic effective oppression, on the other. And since both kinds of people had power, the fate of censorship swayed with the shifts in influence of the two factions. In the extreme, we have Tseretelli trying to hold back the flood with a few chips of wood, knowing what sort of policy has to be followed but being unable to follow it. The image Trotsky uses is that the man who yells "Help!" as he is drowning has the right answer, too, for all the good having the right answer does him.

Thus there are three elements involved in the attribution of a causal characterization to a social system. The first element is whether as an institution it has a solidly institutionalized purpose, from which one can predict its behavior, or whether instead its behavior is erratic and purposeless, and so tends to sap human commitment to it and irritate the people it deals with. The second element is whether the cognitive analysis of the problem prevalent in the institution is of such a character as can come to the right answer, or whether instead the answers are predetermined and therefore necessarily do not recruit their own future support by success when applied to situations in which they give the wrong result. The third element, contributing to both of the previous ones, is whether within the institution power is so distributed that the purposes of certain individuals or groups can determine policy over the long run, and whether it is so distributed so as to give the right answer to a particular situation a reasonable chance of winning.

When a social system is not set up so that its purposes are solidly institutionalized, possible, and backed by an internal distribution of power that makes them stably institutionalized, then its purposes together with the situation are not enough to explain its behavior. In that case, we need a causal characterization that goes beyond describing the group as an actor. That is, the answer to these three questions is an answer to whether or not the social system in question is an actor, with purposes and competences that will explain its behavior, or whether instead it is a social field, a system of balanced or erratic causes whose dispositional properties have to be analyzed. Most historians can deal with groups which are actors. The distinctive thing about de Tocqueville is that he can also deal with a censorship system which is not really an actor, and that about Trotsky that he is not in the least bewildered or surprised when Kerensky follows contradictory policies in the army. But again, when confronted by a social system that is no longer a purposeful entity, both men tend to break it down into its purposeful components and look at what these components think, what resources they have, and what ends they pursue.

## PRINCIPLES OF CUMULATIVE CAUSATION

Neither of these techniques of inference, diagnosing causation from cross-sectional variation or diagnosing the predispositions of a system, is distinctive of history. These are exactly the techniques of inference that Lazarsfeld has formalized in a number of places—the routine tools of the social scientist. Discovering that de Tocqueville and Trotsky use them as well merely confirms a long methodological tradition; it gives us some confidence that these gifted literary figures are scientists (like you and me in principle if a bit more ingenious), and it gives us some confidence that the principles worked out by quantitative types of social scientists are equally applicable to qualitative work.

But there are two types of causal analyses that both de Tocqueville and Trotsky carry out that are not, I believe, in the routine methodological armory of the social sciences: I will call the first the "principle of cumulative causation" and the second the method of "analyzing virtual choices." Both of these are, I believe, closely connected to the method of ideal types and cast some new light on what ideal types are supposed to do in a causal analysis.

By the principle of cumulative causation I mean that both de Tocqueville and Trotsky sort causes of social phenomena into two classes, those that cumulate or grow and those that are random turbulence, quickly sinking back into the general flow of events so that their effects are shortly extinguished. They are particularly interested in cumulative processes, which have some chance of adding up to a permanent change in the nature of a social system. Both of them particularly war against the fashion of historical interpretation which observes a big change (e.g., from a Tsarist to a Soviet type of government), and looks around for a big enough event to cause such a big change, for instance a conspiratorial party which, by enormous bad luck for the society, happened to be smart enough to take power in October 1917. Both believe that large changes in social structures like those carried out by the French and Russian revolutions are built out of what Trotsky liked to call "molecular processes."

Whenever a principle of cumulative causation results in the transformation of a social structure from one with one series of characteristics (e.g., a "feudal method of administration") into one with another series of characteristics (e.g., a "centralized royal bureaucratic method of administration"), then each series of characteristics is an "ideal type" which is related to the other by the inherent, or scientific, connection with the transformative process. That is, the connection between feudal administration and royal bureaucratic administration in de Tocqueville is not merely that a bunch of causes happened to institute one of these and not the other in the eighteenth century in France, and each might have had different characteristics and the whole analysis still be, in principle, the same. Instead there is a causal process, the growth of royal authority and the attempt by the king to bring administrative authorities under his command, and his command out from under the authority of the law and the courts, which tends to transform one system into the other. In this case, then, ideal types are the end states of a causal process and take on their meaning from that process.

By the method of analyzing virtual choices, I mean constructing from the concrete historical materials a more or less complete set of alternative lines of action, as they appeared to the participants in the process. For example, given that the Kadets and the Bolsheviks refused all through the Revolution (with minor exceptions lasting at most a few days) to be in the same government with one another, there were basically only five possible governments: the Kadets and their allies alone, the Bolsheviks and their allies alone, and three alternative types of government including the compromisers, i.e., those willing to be in a government with both, compromisers alone, compromisers and Bolsheviks, and compromisers and Kadets. This, so to speak, delimits the field of choice within which individual people have to make their own choices and within which ultimately "history" must make a choice. During the first part of the revolution, the Soviets represented the compromisers-with-Bolsheviks choice, and the Provisional Government represented the compromisers-with-Kadets choice. By October, the Soviets represented the Bolsheviks-alone choice, the Provisional Government represented the compromisers-alone choice, and in certain parts of the army and in pheripheral areas there were structures representing the Kadets-

alone choice. The revolutionary process was in large measure the transformation of one set of choices, the dual power situation of two governments, both with compromisers in them but neither able to absorb or
defeat the other, into the second situation of choice, in which a Soviet
government dominated by the Bolsheviks confronts the Provisional
Government shorn of bourgeois support and shorn of Bolshevik support. So to some degree we are dealing here with the first kind of ideal
type, one in which two structures are distinguished because they are the
end-states of a transformation process. But these have the additional
causal character of being alternatives concretely posed to the actors on
the scene by the historical situation. Thus the Bolshevik party divides in-
ternally in different ways at different times among the alternative governments that include them and about what attitude to take toward
those dual powers that do not (and presumably cannot) include them.
The compromisers vacillate between the two types of effective government available to them, end up with the only impossible alternative in
the set, and divide decisively at that point into those willing to form part
of a government as allies of the Bolsheviks and those unwilling to do so.
These are, then, typological constructions that have the properties of
being psychologically and socially real alternatives to the people involved and of exhausting the relevant part of social reality, in the sense
that no other choices are likely to be causally effective or made by large
numbers of people.

To summarize the contrasts between the ideal types serving these
different analytical functions, then: (a) the principle of cumulation ideal
type need not be psychologically real, need not be part of the minds of
the participants, while the virtual choice type does need to be real to the
people who make the choice; (b) the former ideal type must describe a
set of variables (characterizing a structure) which are simultaneously
transformed by a causal process of a cumulative or self-reinforcing sort,
while the latter ideal type need be neither the end nor the beginning of
such a process; (c) a virtual choice ideal type must be part of a set of
type-concepts which exhausts the relevant psychological reality of the set
of people who will make the choice, while the cumulative causation type
need only be a part of a set of two which specify each end of the transformative process; (d) because cumulative causal processes between
self-maintaining end states are presumably of relatively few kinds, and
show much less historical variability than the contents of men's minds,
cumulative causation ideal types tend to be more abstract and shorn of
historical content, while virtual choice types tend to have much more
historical specificity; and (e) at least for short-run interpretation, a virtual
choice ideal type need be neither an empirically possible type nor even

one which can remain for a long time stably in men's minds—it can have internal tensions either as a social structure or as a mental structure which prevent it from maintaining itself—while the end points of a causal process, of course, have to exist in the real world to be of any analytical use and are much less conceptually useful if they are evanescent, unstable intermediate states through which the world passes on the wing.

What, then, are the kinds of things that can cumulate in the studies of these men? First, there are individual competences. Trotsky prefers to interpret the shift of mass loyalties to the Bolsheviks as a molecular process of learning the right answer; de Tocqueville thinks that participation in the administration of public affairs cumulates in civic competence in the population and consequently that the divorce of a group from participation explains incapacity and utopianism. Second, administrative and other communications channels necessary for carrying out a particular task collectively agreed upon tend to grow, tests and criteria of performance for roles tend to be developed, bases of trust between people laid down, and in general the social mechanisms by which collective purposes get carried out to improve over time. The capacity of the Soviets, and of the Bolsheviks through the Soviets, to arrange the disposition of troops loyal to them grew over time; the control of local tax collectors by the *Intendent* grew over time. Third, both men see a tendency of governments which *can* expand their powers into new areas to do so, presumably in part because there is almost always *some* advantage to be got by running things, in part because an autonomous niche in the ecology of the political system is a potential breeding ground for hostile organisms and for interference with policies in the rest of the jurisdiction, and in part simply because it takes much smaller causes to get a social organization to do something it can do than something it cannot yet do.

Thus, when Trotsky sees the Soviets in the early part of the revolution taking over various reins of local administration left slack by the destruction of Tsarist administration and trying (under the leadership of the compromisers, the Social Revolutionaries especially) to find someone to turn that power over to, he finds this situation a natural result of the fact that the Soviets can administer, having the consent of the population, while other agencies cannot; when de Tocqueville finds that the progress of civilization creates governmental tasks which the main healthy organ of feudal administration, the *parlements* or high courts, could not do because they were bound by precedent, he finds it natural that the royal bureaucracy should grow into those areas. Fourth, both men frequently make use of a cumulative causal model of growing incompetence—the *parlements* just mentioned are an example—which takes the form of not keeping up with social change because of structural rigidities. That is, as the problems change and develop, only those organizations which can change and develop with them can continue to provide solutions, and hence to maintain authority. The image of the progessive sapping of the authority in the Old Regime, common to the two men, is largely based on this sort of cumulative causal process.

To these more or less straightforward cumulative processes, both men are required in addition, by the nature of their subject matter, to explain growing hostility between social groups. In de Tocqueville, this produces nearly as many contradictions and reckless historical statements as his necessity to find a feudal regime to praise. I believe this is attributable mainly to the difficulty that the social groups which became hostile to each other were actually formed only during the Revolution itself and that France at the end of the Old Regime was not in fact any more shot through with social tensions than it was, say, at the beginning of the eighteenth century. That is, I think de Tocqueville required himself to explain a fact that was not there, which quite often leads people into difficulties. Trotsky's theory is both more explicit and considerably less easy to find fault with, so I will illustrate the conceptual structure with this.

The first part of the theory has to do with the structural preconditions of intense class conflict, not with explaining why there was more social conflict in Russia before the Revolution than in other places (though this might also be true), but rather why the potentiality for a deep revolutionary class conflict was there. This is the theory he calls the "theory of combined and uneven development." In sketchy form, it says that three ways of organizing society have become archaic and no longer viable, because they cannot solve people's problems and consequently cannot maintain authority. These three are (a) the absolutist state where the ruling economic interest is property in land and unfree labor on the land—i.e., absolutist "feudalism," which was therefore replaced in the more advanced countries by bourgeois parliamentarism and a free peasantry; (b) colonial capitalism with foreign domination of the governments of backward countries, without national independence or with fictional national independence, and government-managed, exporting monopolistic business as the ruling economic interest; and (c) parliamentary industrial capitalism with national independence, parliamentary government, wage labor in privately owned factories as the main labor relation, and the native bourgeoisie as the ruling economic interest. None of these three forms of government or modes of production is supposed to be viable in the modern world because none can solve the problems posed by organizing the world in its way. But England and France, at least, do not add to the impossibility of industrial capitalism, also the impossibility of lack of political independence and the impossibility of trying to run a modern country with serf labor.

But Russia was an extraordinarily fragile social system (as was Austria–Hungary) because it combined all three impossibilities: Its modern sector was heavily dominated by foreign capital and its policies closely tied to the policies of the alliance; its pattern of land tenure and organization of agriculture still had a great many feudal elements, high concentration of land with little rural wage labor; its government was not even legitimized by bourgeois democratic methods, let alone by its capacity to solve the problem of proletarian alienation; in fact, it combined the difficulty of being dominated by foreigners with the difficulty of trying to maintain its own domination over minority ethnic groups. This compounding of the problems of development took concrete form in the insertion into the Russian social structure of several kinds of upper classes: a noble and bureaucratic class resting on rural property and nonwage work by peasants; a developing bourgeoisie and political elite in the dominated Central Asian, Caucasian, Baltic, and Balkan nationalities; an industrial bourgeoisie of native Russian production; a foreign banking and investment community with a *comprador* bourgeoisie working for them.

But the political requisites of the forms of domination suitable for each of these types of upper class are in part incompatible. Thus they are only precariously political allies of one another. Further, the forms of oppression compound one another in particular circumstances, as when a feudal landlord commences to regard his feudal privileges exclusively from the point of view of how to extract the greatest commercial profit from them, so that they have neither the legitimacy normal to feudal and traditional relations nor the legitimacy of the "freedom" of a modern worker to move from job to job. Thus the hold of the upper classes on government is precarious and shot through with conflicting interests, and the consent of the laboring classes is precarious because new oppressions are being added onto the old.

Given this brief summary of what was already a brief summary of a previous book of Trotsky's (see "Peculiarities of Russia's Development," *HRR*, I, pp. 3–15), Trotsky then undertakes to explain the cumulative intensification of this latent exacerbated conflict in the rest of the three volumes. Much of the explanation is implicit in the quotations brought forward for various purposes in this chapter, but a summary might go like this: In politics, hostility is directed toward people who try to keep a group from constructing a social system or following a policy that they think is possible and beneficial to them. During a revolution, there is an explosion of possibilities, an explosion of political groups advocating those possibilities in various localities or in various parts of the society. And at the same time, the cover of legality is taken off of the social mechanisms which ordinarily limit possibilities and make things seem inevitable—the police, the army, and property relations. This means that to stop someone from constructing an alternative social order one has actually to go out and stop him—to rally those whose interests are touched by the question, organize them into an effective force, come to a consensus on policy, and act. That is, class relations are stripped, rendered naked, and hence visible. And the bourgeois that wants to institute regular production under his ownership is doing so against an apparent real possibility of doing so under the workers' ownership.

In such a situation of Hobbesian group conflict, several things happen. The first is that people on all sides stop listening to empty rhetoric about the principles of government and preserving socialist legality and supporting the allies "insofar as" their aims are democratic—rhetoric which refuses to address the question of who is going to get what, and when. The second is that people either structurally or psychologically ambivalent (Trotsky calls them petty bourgeois, but he ends up calling everybody who took an ambivalent position petty bourgeois, regardless of class origins) tend to withdraw from the conflict, since they have no opinion about whether the Bolsheviks or the Kadets should win—they had in mind Kerensky. The third is a very close identification of the policy one advocates and the question of power, of the organization of the state and the disposition of troops. Many fewer people in a revolution advocate worker's control of industry but do not follow this by advocating that the workers take the factories and defend them. And this in turn means that all political conflicts tend to turn into military conflicts rather than parliamentary debates, with all the exacerbation of hostility that tends to accompany the experience of being shot at.

The revolution itself, then, is the furnace within which classes are formed, class lines drawn, class hostilities intensified. And classes form through the formation of parties, draw lines at party boundaries, and intensify conflicts because they are fighting for power.

There are two different types of cumulative causation involved here. The first has to do with the cumulative insertion of Russia into the international capitalist system, with the consequent commercialization of her feudalism and colonialization of her commerce. This cumulative process of involvement with a developing world-system inserts tensions into the social system which are difficult to resolve with the mechanisms of that system. Thus there is a specific kind of cumulation of incapacity, in which the new problems are inserted into the system by powerful outside forces; and the incapacity has to do in part with conflicts within the upper classes about how to get the poor to work for them and how to provide the political preconditions for that work.

The second kind of cumulation has to do with the difference in the learning process between "normal" circumstances and revolution. In normal circumstances, the bourgeoisie do not take their property directly away from possessing workers. The property is not in the workers' hands, and it is the law in its majestic equality that keeps it out of their hands. Workers learn that life is hard, that the race is not to the swift, and perhaps in an extremity of radicalism, that "the law, sir, is an ass." But the worker does not learn that the man in the big house in the next street is his enemy. In revolutionary cumulation, the ambivalent and the weak drop out of the fray, leaving the field to the strong parties that know what they want.

Both of these illustrate a main feature of Trotsky's analysis, which differentiates him from de Tocqueville and from most other historians and social scientists: his extreme sensitivity to conditions leading to different rates and directions of change. The army moves slower than the proletariat; Russia's class tensions grow at a higher speed than England's or Germany's; people who are ambivalent drop out of politics faster in time of revolution than in normal times; the peasantry grows toward anarchic disorganization of the administrative and property system, while the proletariat grows toward the capacity to take power; the masses grow more radical while their leaders elected a few weeks before either grow more conservative, or do not grow radical as fast. That is, Trotsky thinks quite naturally in the form of differential equations, in which the dependent variable is not the *value* of another variable, but a *rate of change* of that variable; and the causal conditions he is looking for are not associated with high values of the dependent variable, but instead with high rates of change. Note that this is not the causally thin stuff of the Club of Rome, enchanted to discover that a constant percentage rate of change gives rise to an exponential curve; instead it is about what causes some exponentials to go up faster than others or in different directions. The pulse or event conception of cause, popularized by Hume and by the psychological experiment, fits very uncomfortably with Trotsky's mode of analysis. There is no event that causes the army to be less ready to go into rebellion than the workers, but "molecular processes" of contrasting speeds.

These cumulative processes, both those common to the two writers and those which distinguish Trotsky, give rise to analytical ideal types that represent the end states, the places where the process starts and the places where it ends. The cumulation of individual learning yields a competent population, one that knows how to solve political problems, while a population whose learning has been stunted by detachment from politics (or by too much exposure to petty bourgeois vaporings) is politically incompetent, idealistic, and inclined to favor wild schemes that will not actually solve the problems. There is a remarkable similarity in the tone of contempt with which de Tocqueville speaks of the political thinkers of the Enlightenment and that with which Trotsky talks about the enlightened circles of the center parties in Russia a century and a half later.

> Our revolutionaries had the same fondness for broad generalizations, cut-and-dried legislative systems, and a pedantic symmetry; the same contempt for hard facts; the same taste for reshaping institutions on novel, ingenious, original lines....Even the politicians' phraseology was borrowed largely from the books they read; it was cluttered up with abstract words, gaudy flowers of speech, sonorous clichés, and literary turns of phrase [ORR, p. 147].

And after a great deal of progress of civilization:

> The cumbersome and good-for-nothing state apparatus, representing a combination of March socialist with tzarist bureaucrat, was perfectly accommodated to the task of self-deception. The half-baked March socialist dreaded to appear to the bureaucrat a not wholly mature statesman. The bureaucrat dreaded lest he show a lack of respect to the new ideas. Thus was created a web of official lies, in which generals, district attorneys, newspaper-men, commissars, aides-de-camp, lied the more, the nearer they stood to the seats of power. The commander of the Petrograd military district made comforting reports, for the reason that Kerensky, faced by an uncomforting reality, had great need of them....Thus the rosy March nimbus had turned into a gray vapor, hiding the actual traits of things [HRR, III, p. 204].

Likewise an administrative organization with consensus on operating procedures, well-defined roles, and efficient internal communications is the long-run result of undertaking tasks in common. De Tocqueville pictures the nobility and monasteries uninformed about the state of the peasants because they were no longer in administrative contact with them, while the parish clergy knew them well, and the Intendent had multiple reliable communications channels. Trotsky contrasts the Soviets conquering power but not knowing what to do with it at the beginning of the revolution, with the quiet, coordinated confidence of the October coup d'etat.

The administration which has not yet filled its niche is contrasted to that which fills the whole society. The organization perfectly capable of running a feudal army fails against the modern Hohenzollern army. The modern bourgeois republics of France and England manage their internal tensions, while backward Russian society bursts apart, with contending upper classes and raging lower classes. Rosy March speechmaking turns into gray civil war in October.

In each case, then, there is both an ideal type that corresponds to a social structure before the cumulation takes place and another ideal type that corresponds to a structure that comes after. The later type is crucial, because it is the historical deposit that the cumulative process leaves behind. Weber's ideal type of bureaucracy was such an analytical ideal type, being the end of a process in which rationalization of administration is undertaken by a monocratic authority.

## VIRTUAL CHOICE

When Max Weber wanted to interpret rational and systematic work in a bourgeois calling, he did so by showing that it made sense in terms either of gaining prestige in a Protestant sect organization or of gaining salvation in a Calvinist theology modified into a popular ethical religion. That is, when we observe that people choose a specific pattern of behavior, we may guess that they do it because they are making a virtual choice, a choice inside the mind, of a certain meaning system in terms of which that chosen activity makes sense. Weber outlined various varieties of church organization that more or less closely approximated that kind of organization that would maximize the motivation for rational accomplishment in the world, and various variants of Protestant theology that more or less closely approximated that kind which would maximize the ethical imperatives and rewards for such behavior. These are full of historical specificity; Weber has to know specifically what the Pietists thought, how the Quakers were organized, whether the Lutheran idea of a calling in the world was ethically hooked up to salvation in as close a way as it was in popular Calvinism, and so on. The reason is that while one can outline abstractly the sort of sect organization and theology that would maximize psychological pressures on the ethics of parishioners, such an ideal type is of no particular use in historical analysis because there is no inherent causal process tending to produce such a church organization. If the Quakers come very close to the maximum ideal type of sect but have an illuminationist theology rather than a popular Calvinist one, that is just tough. It is the concrete historical reality of the extreme sect organization combined with the wrong kind of theology, while the Calvinist theology in many places was associated with a commercial aristocracy and nonegalitarian congregational organizations approaching a church, that are the actual motivating forces in the choice of a rational bourgeois calling. That is, unless it is in the mind of every member of the congregation that he can be an ethical example, the motivational force of an ethical system is reduced. And unless ethical perfection is closely tied by the theology to the reward of salvation, the motivational force of the ethical system is also reduced. But it would be of little use to Weber to construct an ideal type of Quakerlike sect organization and Calvinist theology, because there just were not any such entities around to be motivating people to bourgeois accomplishments.

Furthermore, bureaucracies tend to be produced in a wide variety of societies in a wide variety of areas of life, in armies and corporations and tax-collecting agencies, in absolute monarchies and modern democracies and communist autocracies. But Calvinist theology, with all its purported consequences for capitalism, happened only once in one cultural area. Thus the ideal types of Calvinist ethical pressures, or (to a lesser extent) of sect organization, play an analytical role completely different from that of the ideal type of bureaucracy. The first kind is built up of the materials that are in men's minds, the second is built up of the consequences of systematic cumulative processes.

Similarly, when de Tocqueville explains the adoption of Roman law, the characteristics are those of a historical public opinion:

> These causes do not suffice to explain the simultaneous introduction of Roman law into every continental country. I think the singular availability of the Roman law—which was a slave law—for the purposes of monarchs, who were just then establishing their absolute power upon the ruins of the old liberties of Europe, was the true cause of the phenomenon. The Roman law carried civil society to perfection, but it invariably degraded political society, because it was the work of a highly civilized and thoroughly enslaved people. Kings naturally embraced it with enthusiasm, and established it wherever they could throughout Europe [ORR, p. 223].

Consider what might have been an ideal type of a legal and political cultural system which simultaneously resolves disputes between citizens in a "fair" way, a way that will be acceptable to them and that will produce social peace and let private functions be done efficiently, and which resolves disputes between the monarch and citizens in favor of the monarch. We could develop a set of characteristics of systems that would tend to be maximized, given a "molecular process" motivated by forces tending to produce civil peace and monarchic power. According to de Tocqueville in this passage, such a process would tend to produce a law with characteristics that distinguish Roman law from "Germanic" feudal law. But that kind of ideal type construction is not what de Tocqueville was up to. Instead he was characterizing two systems that were historically present at the time his monarchs were choosing, Roman law and "Germanic" law, historically present in the sense that there were trained lawyers available ("Monarchs who have trampled the laws have almost always found a lawyer ready to prove the lawfulness of their acts—to establish learnedly that violence was just, and that the oppressed were in the wrong [ORR, pp. 223–224]"), that the law was already partially institutionalized in the church in Canon Law, that the people so trained were not people of independent power but could be hired by the royal bureaucracy, and so on. It might well be that if they instead had been offered the option of adopting a Byzantine caesaropapism or Confucian filial piety, they might have preferred them to Roman law. But those alternatives were not socially and psychologically present, so the ideal type of "slave law" gets filled with the concrete historical content of "Roman law" in explaining late medieval and early modern developments in Western Europe.

> But the [early revolutionary] period of universal and indiscriminate embraces does not last long. The class struggle dies down at the beginning of a revolution only to come to life afterward in the form of civil war. In the faery—like rise of compromisism is contained the seed of its inevitable fall. The official French journalist, Claude Anet, explained Kerensky's swift loss of popularity by a lack of tact which impelled the socialist politican to actions "little harmonizing" with his role. "He frequents the imperial loges, he lives in the Winter Palace... he sleeps in the bed of the Russian emperiors. A little too much vanity and vanity a little too noticeable...." Tact implies, in the small as well as the great, an understanding of the situation and of one's place in it. Of this understanding Kerensky had not a trace. Lifted up by the trustful masses, he was completely alien to them, did not understand, and was not the least interested in, the question of how the revolution looked to them and what inferences they were drawing from it. The masses expected bold action from him, but he demanded from the masses that they should not interfere with his magnanimity and eloquence [HRR, II, p. 137].

Here the concrete historical content is even more obvious because it has the proper name of Kerensky. But Trotsky is also trying to explain why the symbol which saved the government toward the beginning of the Revolution, the entry of Kerensky and some other socialists into ministries, lost its capacity to elicit loyalty by midsummer. So he has to analyze Kerensky as a psychological entity in the minds of the masses: What does he look like to them? In particular, does he look like a socialist leader? And more particularly, though at this point implicitly, does he look as much like a socialist leader as the incoming president of the Petrograd Soviet, Trotsky, the revolutionary puritan? Does he show that "understanding of the situation and one's place in it" which makes a symbol attract loyalty rather than grate on the nerves?

Though it is implicit here, Kerensky as a person has to be stripped of many of his characteristics, to be reduced from a whole man who puts on his pants one leg at a time to a public symbol whose few psychologically present characteristics are then compared with a model of what a socialist leader should look like. That is, Kerensky is here being forced to play the same analytical role as Roman law in de Tocqueville's brief characterization, or the methods by which the visible church recognized the invisible church of predestined saints in Calvinist sects in such a way as to promote ethical self control in daily life in Weber's.

There are actually three intellectual processes embedded in such analyses, but they are buried under the apparent dependence of the whole analysis on proper names, so that their abstract character gets lost. The first is the extraction from the historical individual (Calvinist theology or Quaker sect organization, Roman law, Kerensky) of those characteristics that are causally relevant. Which these are will depend on who historically is making the choice. For Weber, the relevant characteristics were selected on the ground of maximizing ethical discipline in this-worldly pursuits; for de Tocqueville, maximizing usefulness in the subjection of feudal powers to absolute monarchs; for Trotsky, maximizing trust of the masses in a socialist leader. In doing this, all three start with the dependent behavior, the character of the choice which one wants to explain. All three then derive, more or less intuitively or explicitly, the set of characteristics that will maximize the likelihood, among the historically acting subjects, of the choice of interest. Weber studies the kinds of organization of Quakers and other sects that will maximize the choice of ethical imperatives from the religion in the governance of activities in daily life, and the ideal type of sect is derived from these. Trotsky studies what sort of responsiveness to the masses would maximize the likelihood of those masses choosing to trust the leader. De Tocqueville much more implicitly presumes that there must be characteristics of Roman law produced by the interests of the Roman emperor that would maximize its usefulness to aspiring absolute monarchs. Then the concrete historical entity is looked at from the point of view of this maximizing ideal type. The reason we are interested in how far the Quakers came from having the ideal theology for maximizing ethical self-discipline, or how far the Calvinists came from having the ideal type of sect organization, is that those departures decrease the causal force for ethical discipline. The reason Kerensky's departure from socialist tact is relevant is that it causes socialist sentiments to be less readily called up as a source of loyalty by the provisional government.

Thus the first step is the transformation of the concrete historical entity into a position along a variable. The method of doing this is to imagine a historical entity which would maximize the causal impact on the psychology of the relevant group, the Calvinist group with the least "church" and the most "sectarian" organization, the revolutionary puritan, the slave law. Then the concrete historical entity is, intuitively, measured against this abstract maximizing ideal type and judged pretty close or pretty far away. From being a concrete man, Kerensky becomes an abstract position on a psychological scale among the masses, a revolutionary fop.

The second step is to construct the field of choice. That is, Roman law for de Tocqueville is neither the most slave of all slave laws nor the most civil of all civil laws. What is crucial is that it is more careful of civil peace and more reckless of powers that stand against the monarch than the feudal "Germanic" legal tradition, and its lawyers were more dependent on the king than were the nobility who administered feudal law. That is, the relative distance of feudal law and Roman law from the ideal typical slave law is the crucial thing, not how far Roman law might be from the Byzantine court of Muscovy or from some other entity not historically present. Weber, in spite of noble efforts on his part, never managed to make clear to his critics what were the alternatives to "rational bourgeois capitalism" and "systematic ethical achievement in a wordly calling." It was *ethically uninformed* capitalism, capitalism wedded to the good life of the Italian city aristocracy, to conquering Indian gold mines in Peru in *condottierri* capitalism, to undisciplined greed or political capitalism without rational productive enterprise. The grand mistake of most Weber's critics was to believe that he was talking about the choice of capitalism over feudalism instead of the choice of industrial capitalism over commercial and military capitalism. But their projection of their own interests onto Weber does not prevent Weber's own description of the alternative to "the spirit of capitalism" being perfectly clear. And the recurrent description of the grays and browns of the Soviet in contrast to the bright clothes of the provisional government in Trotsky makes it clear where the psychological alternative to Kerensky was likely to be found.

The third part of the analysis, then, is to describe the division of the population (or of the relevant actors if they are corporate) by their choices among these alternatives. It is, of course, exposure to near to the maximum pressure, in Protestant sects or Calvinist churches, that

Weber thought would produce ethical self-discipline in a wordly calling, so Quakers and Puritans should be especially prominent in industrial production, less prominent in commerce, especially warlike commerce such as slave trading or exploitation of conquered gold mines. It is the kings who choose Roman law, the nobility who prefer feudal or customary laws. It is the workers and soldiers who lose faith in Kerensky, while the bourgeoisie find him a fine figure of a socialist, if one has to have socialists.

## CONCLUSIONS

There is more to de Tocqueville and Trotsky than their near approach to Lazarsfeld and Weber in their methods. In particular, both of them had fairly clear notions about what it took to make a social system viable under specific historical circumstances.

What can we reasonably be said to have demonstrated so far? First, we tried to illustrate that de Tocqueville and Trotsky converged on a similar analysis of the same phenomenon by outlining the common theory of authority and its decay in the two men. This gives presumptive evidence that they must have arrived at this theory by a common method, since their prejudices about what kinds of authorities there ought to be and what they ought to do to maintain themselves were about as near to opposite as we can find. The question then arises, what are these methods?

Second, we have tried to demonstrate that both Trotsky and de Tocqueville used conventional sociological methods, though mostly without numbers and with somewhat more attention to whether their categories of the population made substantive sense than we are used to seeing. They traced causation by studying covariation of dependent and independent variables and by studying the predisposition of social systems producing distinctive incompetence—even as you and I.

Third, we can claim to have demonstrated that they both also used two methods of ideal-type analysis, the first, in which the ideal type represent end points of a cumulative causal process, and the second, in which they represent virtual psychological alternatives for a population, between which the population can be conceived as choosing. Both of these kinds of ideal types were also developed and discussed by Max Weber, so again we find nothing fundamentally new in the method. But we do find that the innovations of Weber are necessary, that it would be very difficult to write either de Tocqueville's or Trotsky's books without a pretty good command of ideal-type methodology. I believe that much of the superiority of Trotsky over de Tocqueville has to do with the greater facility with which he handles this methodology, a greater facility he probably learned more from Marx than from anyone else (as did, I believe, Weber).

# 3

# Functional Analysis of Class Relations in Smelser and Bendix

## SMELSER'S ARGUMENT

The overall intellectual problems of Neil Smelser's *Social Change in the Industrial Revolution* and Reinhard Bendix's *Work and Authority in Industry*[1] are quite similar, the development of the role of industrial worker, especially his role in class conflict.

Smelser approaches the problem as one of social differentiation. The idea is that different aspects of, for example, the production of cotton cloth need to be governed by different normative systems. The selection of an amount of cloth to be produced needs to be governed by the amount of demand at different prices, so the normative and reward system bearing on that decision ought to be set up so that prices and quantities are the decisive consideration. The activity of producing the cloth on a machine, on the other hand, ought to be governed by norms of skill, of steady disciplined work, of a fair day's work for a fair day's pay, and so on. The normative and reward system governing the worker's role should therefore be oriented to rewarding and developing skill and discipline and taking decent care of the worker's family.

[1]Hereafter referred to as *SCIR* and *WAI*, respectively. Bibliographical details are provided in the references.

If we find that weaving is organized in family enterprises, one and the same authority and reward system decides how much should be produced at different prices and how skill, discipline, and a well-supported family should be obtained. In that case, the amount produced will be influenced by considerations of family welfare, considerations of preparing the children for adult jobs, and the like. A family of weavers cannot easily shut down for the winter and open up again in the spring in response to demand. The kids get hungry. The family-organized part of the economy does not adjust production quickly to variations in market price.

Exactly similar considerations affect the family's level of investment. A family of weavers perhaps ought to buy a steam-driven machine, but their savings and investment are governed by family considerations as well as industrial productivity. When the choice is between a steam engine and repairing the roof out of limited savings, the norms of rational adaptation of capital to production are interfered with by norms about staying warm and dry.

One of the things that the industrial revolution was about was the growth of separate structures governed by separate norms for these distinct activities: Worker welfare was secured by a moral structure (by families) different from market responsiveness (by firms), and rational investment in capital equipment by still different moral and organizational arrangements (by banks) from market responsiveness.

The process of creating these separate moral systems and their organizational carriers is one of changing the behavior, and the conception of appropriate behavior, of a large number of men. Naturally, a weaver mainly worried about feeding his family through the winter and keeping a roof over their heads is likely to be suspicious of a move to set up a social structure of firms and banks that is specifically designed not to care about his welfare. A casual reading of the evidence shows that he was quite right to be suspicious. Such a structural differentiation "needs" to develop an alternative moral order which does care about the welfare of his family and the training of his children, now that market responsiveness and capital investment no longer are managed by structures that are supposed to care. But there is no inherent necessity that a social structure will do what is "needed."

Smelser's argument about how such reorganizations of the normative system takes place has two parts, one about values and one about processes. The value part is that such reorganizations cannot take place unless there are "higher" values beyond those embedded in the present structure, for instance values of "productivity" or "progress." Since clearly some things that were valuable were previously done by family enterprise, which the new firms and banks do not propose to do, the legitimacy of the firms and banks depends on the legitimacy of what they *are* needed for. If responsiveness to the market is needed less than security of weavers' families, if production wasted because the weaver bought a roof instead of a steam engine is not needed, then the differentiation tends not to take place. Only if the general values make the achievements of the new structure more valuable than the achievements of the old will the process of differentiation take place.

But given this requirement that the values generally favor the new over the old, what is actually required to develop factories and banks is a cause of comparable complexity to the effect to be explained. Factories do not spring full blown from the value of progress. In fact, a factory is quite a complicated thing to cause, and a lot of very good men with a lot of money have failed at it, though they have worked very hard at it. The problem, then, is how to explain how something as vague as a value for productivity could cause something as specific and complicated as a worker role differentiated from management and investment, with these latter also developed into appropriate complex managing and banking roles. Smelser needs a process by which, so to speak, a cause can grow gradually until it is suitable to cause the complicated thing that can achieve the value which sets the whole thing off.

The theoretical procedure he uses can be summarized for our purposes as follows. In order to cause a reorganization of roles, one needs the following components: a dissatisfaction with present arrangements (which must be diagnosed as such in terms of the value system); ideas about what to do about it; money and other powers committed to those ideas; specific functioning social organizations, with the bugs worked out, that use the powers to implement the ideas; and a competitive driving out of the old practices to be replaced by the new, more satisfactory ones. There is a certain loose sense in which each stage of this process requires successful accomplishment of the previous one. One cannot spend money on an idea yet to be thought of; one cannot compete with hand-loom weavers with an investment not yet arranged into power looms operated by factory workers. We can therefore arrange our analysis of the growth of a cause by analogy with the growth of a product in production, which, for example, starts off as raw cotton, becomes combed cotton, becomes thread, becomes cloth, becomes clothes. Each stage is required before the next is reached; each stage is an increasingly specific product for increasingly specific uses. A blue jumper is, in a very general way, partly caused by the combing of cotton, but needs many stages of increasingly specific value added before that cause becomes specific enough to cause a blue jumper. Likewise, the general value of productivity needs a series of stages of increasingly specific developments before it can become a cause of a factory worker running an automatic loom.

Each of these stages of the growth of a cause in its turn has distinct moral requirements and human side-effects. A general perception that the performance of a social system does not live up to generally accepted values, before there are any real ideas about how to solve the problem, tends to produce wild ideas, to produce, for example, blame that does not fit with the existing role system because no one is specifically required to do some specific thing about the dissatisfaction. Such wild ideas and "senseless" aggression "need" to be controlled, so they do not damage a system which, if bad, is still the best we have. Or second, a period of seeking new ideas would be discouraged by applying too strict criteria of profit and loss, and rather requires a morality of "let a thousand flowers bloom," and a reward system emphasizing fame for bright ideas rather than profits from a valuable enterprise. But nine hundred ninety-nine of the flowers are superfluous when an entrepreneur has to decide which kind of a factory to put his money into. The tough muscling out of old fashioned competitors is not usually a matter of friendly encouragement of technical progress, nor yet hopeful investment in a risky enterprise, but rather cold-blooded conquest of a social niche.

In addition to this theory, the book carries (the verb is chosen viciously, but I think correctly) a theory of Parsons about where, in general, distinct moral requirements of roles come from. The idea is that all social systems have pressures on them to set up separate moral systems for deciding what to do (G), for deciding the best way to do it (A), for training and motivating people to do it (L), and for dividing up benefits and power among the people (I). Consequently, systems tend to differentiate along those lines, producing four normative and organizational subsystems. These *subsystems*, then, have four kinds of problems: deciding what to do, how to do it, how to get people to do it, and who benefits. And so on ad infinitem.

But since, for example, one wants to train and motivate people (L) to do what has been decided (G) efficiently (A) and to be motivated by the benefits that are their fair share (I), the training and motivational system needs to have control mechanisms (interchanges) to bring its differentiated moral system into keeping with the requirements of the other subsystems. People need to be trained and motivated to follow decisions (L–G interchange), to work efficiently (L–A interchange), and not to revolt against wage slavery, or at least to do it outside working hours ($L$–$I$ interchange).

Now, naturally, we have to consider the special moral requirements of the job of say, specifying what kinds of authority practices people will be trained for, and what kinds of authority systems will (given the character of the work force) give the top management the highest level of disciplinary power. That is, the interchange itself consists of a set of activities, the activities nowadays concentrated in personnel departments of large firms. Likewise, labor relations and collective bargaining are not merely interchanges between the $I$ system (the wage structure of the firm) and the $L$ system (the families that send the worker off with a bright morning face). They are also activities with special requirements; the fact that the interchange has requirements is shown by the fact that when it is badly done the factory stops in a strike. In summary, differentiation requires integration, integration requires work, and such work itself has distinctive moral requirements.

The sort of evidence given in the book for this superstructure predicting where the fault lines are, along which differentiation will take place, is that when analyzing a differentiation, Smelser can call it by one of the names suggested in this scheme. This is not the kind of evidence I want to examine here. The scheme does not predict specifically enough what kinds of division of labor will *not* take place, and which ones will, so that I can conceive of how I might reject it. At any rate, the possibilities of rejecting this theory are not seriously sought in the book, so its intellectual accomplishment cannot be a testing of this theory in tough tests. I therefore propose to ignore the four functional requirements and the very large number of interchanges they imply.

## FUNCTIONAL EXPLANATION OF CHANGE

There is a strategic ambiguity in the description of the "value added" notion of how a cause grows. Does the reasoning go backward from an observed effect—that, for example, in order to start a savings bank (observed) there has *to have been* a developed idea of what a savings bank would look like? Or does it go forward, so that if a society "needs" savings banks it *will develop* causes sufficient to produce them, including (eventually) developed ideas of what a savings bank should look like? In the old fashioned language, is the development of ideas about savings banks a *necessary precondition* of savings banks, but not itself a *necessary result* of the troubles workers have in matching income and expenditure in an industrial economy? Or are workers' difficulties a sufficient condition of savings banks, a condition which operates by way of developing the other necessary conditions, such as ideas? This strategic ambiguity is characteristic of functional reasoning generally.

In the case of the blue jumper, we know that money paid for the jumper runs backward through the process of production to pay for the combing of the cotton, so we are hardly surprised to find, in the first half of Smelser's book, that people worked hard to find ways to comb enough cotton. When the same logic is applied to people who did not yet know they needed trade unions and savings banks in place of friendly societies, it gets more suspicious. There is no obvious mechanism playing the role of money to translate a future blue jumper into a present cause of combed cotton.

One possible resolution of this ambiguity is a historically specific functionalism *in which the dependent variable is the capacity to differentiate roles*. We observe that in fact the Indian spinning industry of the time did not create spinning factories nor trade unions nor working-class savings banks nor cooperative stores, while Lancastershire did. That must mean that the sufficient conditions for those developments existed in England but not in India. If we imagine that these conditions are social mechanisms facilitating differentiation, then it must be true that English (or at least Manchester) social structure had the functional requirements for change of industrial social structure. If money has to be put into new ideas for social change to take place, then England must have had social mechanisms for putting money into new ideas, and perhaps India not.

An alternative resolution of the ambiguity would be to apply "potential" concepts, like fertility. When we say that a patch of ground in Northern Europe is fertile for wheat, we do not say that somehow or other the genetic stock for wheat originating in the Levant will necessarily make its way down the Mediterranean and then North. Perhaps likewise, when we say that factory operatives can no longer cultivate their gardens when work is slack and so need savings banks, we mean that *if* the seed of savings banks is sown it will produce a lush crop.

Or finally, an alternative imagery is that of accumulated energy, that as the pressure on the working-class family builds up, the dikes of the old structure have to give way somewhere. Parliament and men of goodwill in the upper classes are hydraulic engineers who, if they see the problem in time and are skilled enough at building channels to carry the flood, can save the dikes. But once diverted into savings banks channels, the energy of the flood digs the channel deep.

One purpose of these metaphors is to distract us from the tendency to follow the process of the growth of a cause from a general value of security to a specific provision of savings banks, as if banks were oaks that grow with an inner logic implicit in the acorn. What we have to establish is whether, and how, the previous development of a cause produces the next stage of growth, necessary for that cause to develop into what it in fact became. Insofar as the concepts at each stage are built into general concepts *fitted to the task of explaining the next stage*, the concepts are causally adequate.

The second purpose of the metaphors is to suggest that there are various mechanisms by which a functional theory of social change can be completed. Some of these lead to historically contingent predictions, that if factory labor grows up in a social structure like Northern England, then it will tend to produce savings banks (or functionally equivalent specialized savings structures) while if it grows up elsewhere it may not. Some of the images provide for a good deal of chance in the connection between cause and effect, so that Parliament may succeed in providing channels for worker protest or may go the way of the Paris Parlement and the French king. Some of them provide quite determinate relations between one stage (e.g., dissatisfaction with security of earnings) and the next (e.g., the growth of *some* savings mechanisms).

## "DISTURBANCE"

The most original argument of the book is that "collective behavior" of cotton workers in the first part of the nineteenth century was caused by the necessity to reorganize family roles, brought on by the growth of factory labor separate from the family, and ended when that reorganization had been successfully carried through. By *collective behavior* I mean (following Smelser's definition in his later book, *Theory of Collective Behavior*) behavior organized by "disturbed," "utopian," or "overgeneralized" beliefs. These beliefs are characterized by three major features: (*a*) They are "utopian" in the sense that they promise a resolution to a wide variety of problems by a fundamental social transformation, with the path to that transformation, the social materials out of which the transformation will be built, inadequately specified, and with the causal connections between the transformation and the resulting solutions to problems being left vague; (*b*) they are "disturbed" or "regressive" in a psychoanalytic sense, especially allowing aggression uncontrolled by careful norms of blame and responsibility to be expressed and generally showing weakened control of impulses by culturally approved ego functions (socially instituted standards of what is fair or valuable); and (*c*) they are sporadic, in the sense that when a developed nonutopian and socially controlled solution to the problem which caused the collective behavior is found, they tend to disappear; that is utopian ideas have difficulty competing with ideas integrated into the social structure and the overall value system.

The theory then argues that "disturbed" ideas showing these three characteristics tend to be produced whenever an old (less differentiated) structure no longer performs adequately according to the value system by which it is legitimated, but when adequate ideas, commitment of resources, and routinization of a new solution (the more differentiated structure) have not come about. More briefly, when people have a problem that passionately concerns them but have no sensible answers, they will give foolish answers. While such a scheme does tend to give a historian who knows the sensible answer a sense of self-satisfied complacency watching the scurrying of panicky workers whose nest is disturbed, it is a coherent account of how people's definitions of situations come to have specified characteristics.

Let us now examine a few quotations.

We know but of ONE remedy for the evils of the 'Factory System,' and for the many ills which afflict society—ills so numerous, and of such magnitude, that they force themselves upon the attention at every moment....That remedy is of universal application; we mean EDUCATION [SCIR, p. 287]. III

(See also a similar utopian description of the effects of education and reduced hours for children, pp. 295–296—VI.)

I think [two relays of children] would be very injurious to both master and man; as to workmen, parents cannot keep children without getting them employ; even if it was to purjure themselves, or thereabouts, they must work; they would change about from mills, and go fine counts in the morning and coarse counts in the afternoon, or a cardroom hand would go piecing, and a piecer to card-room; they would work, that's my opinion; and if they had not two places to work at, then the other part of the day they'll be out; then they begin to find delight in all sorts of mischief, and... I think they'll not like to work at all; for children like play and idleness, and getting into mischief. Some boys and girls that are of a wildish nature, if they were to work only six or eight hours a day, would be running away from work altogether. It would never do at all, never [SCIR, p. 240]. II

You (laborers) have received no higher wages, though you may perform the work of ten men; although you may produce ten times the value of your own labor; therefore machinery works against labor....It works for the master, not for the workman [SCIR, p. 255]. II

About one-third of our working population . . . consists of weavers and laborers, whose average earnings do not amount to a sum sufficient to bring up
and maintain their families without parochial assistance. It is this portion of
the community, for the most part decent and respectable in their lives, which
is suffering most from the depression of wages, and the hardship of the times.
It is to this class of my poor fellow creatures, in particular, that I desire to
recommend the system of cooperation, as the only means which, at present,
seem calculated to diminish the evils under which they live [SCIR p. 258]. II

Oastlers dire promise in 1831 that the masters would never stop until the
"manufacture of empire is concentrated under one large roof, and the world
supplied by one gigantic firm. . . .Till human nature is almost physically and
morally destroyed, and all the inhabitants of this land shall be the slaves of
one great manufacturing nabob" [SCIR, p. 288]. II

Most of those attracted to cooperative communities were described as persons
"already degraded by starvation and idleness" and "poets, enthusiasts,
dreamers; reformers of all things, and the baser sorts of disbelievers in any"
[SCIR, p. 380]. VI

What is supposed to be the case is that the quotations marked II show
symptoms of "disturbed" thought, utopian, regressive, and inferior in
competition to the more fully developed thought of those marked III,
and especially VI. But the most uncontrolled aggression seems to me to
be in the last quotation, which is produced by practical cooperative store
people in opposition to the utopian cooperative community people, that
is, at stage VI of differentiation rather than at Stage II. The most utopian
statement seems to me to be that about the wonders of education
(though perhaps I am biased by knowing too much about schools),
which is offered to remind agitators for a 10-hour bill of the value system
they are proposing to violate. The soberest account is the Bolton spinner
discussing what would happen to family authority if children are separated from their parents who are working in the factory, exactly the
separation that Smelser himself argues threw the spinning operators
into a disturbed state. Although the negative utopia of one big factory
with degraded workers is undoubtedly unfair to the tiny capitalists of
those times, and so supports Smelser's hypothesis, the proposal for a
calm consideration of whether hand loom weavers would not be better
off without capitalists in cooperative communities seems to me quite
undisturbed. What happened to handloom weavers under capitalism is
not too far from the negative utopia of Oastler, and the laissez faire
economists who argued that capitalism was really good for them might
well be described by C. Wright Mills' phrase as "utopian capitalists."

My purpose in introducing these quotations is not to point out that a Bolton spinner came much closer to Smelser's analysis of the problem than the parliamentarians in charge of enforcing "realism" on the spinners, though of course I enjoy that incidental result. Instead, I want to point out that the phenomena supposed to occur at one stage of the process of differentiation occur also at other stages, and some phenomena that occur at stage II, "disturbance," are perfectly sober realistic institutional analyses. Since it is being able to predict the content and timing of such outbursts that Smelser urges as the main advantage of his method (see *SCIR*, chapter XIV, pp. 384–401, especially at pp. 388–389, 394, 398–399), this brings into question what has actually been accomplished in the book.

One possible conclusion, of course, is that nothing has been accomplished. Yet the analysis as a whole has a persuasive quality not captured by assuming that, for example, he was trying to specify the conditions under which disturbed, utopian, or aggressive ideas occur. This suggests to me that there is something else in the analysis, *not* specified by the concepts of stages of differentiation, that renders it persuasive. In fact, at the point in the argument at which the Bolton spinner is quoted, the reader says to himself that the quotation shows that Smelser is onto something. The vitriolic attack by the cooperative store people on the cooperative community people occurs in a general context in which we can see why the stores are growing rapidly and cooperative communities declining, to give cooperatives a place in the English economy they were to hold and expand for over a century.

As a subsidiary line of argument to the same effect, that the accomplishment of the book is not what it claims, consider the following quotation about savings banks:

> Thus the paradox: savings banks had their genesis in dissatisfactions with the conditions of the poor; because of the transitional and desperate conditions of the really poor, however, the savings bank could not assist them; yet the banks provided, after all, a cushion of stability in the sphere of consumption and savings for the new, more differentiated elements of industrial society [*SCIR*, p. 375].

That is, the stages of a process of differentiation can change the nature of the original functional dissatisfactions so that it is completed by quite a different set of values from those that started it. But if we have to explain one kind of innovation at the beginning (a structurally differentiated unit that will provide security for marginal displaced groups) and a different kind of innovation at the end (one that will help the lower-middle and upper-working class consolidate their position), the nature of the intervening connections between stages has to be pretty loose. If the Speenhamland system of supplementing poor people's wages to secure a minimum income for them, or encouragement of friendly societies, are "stop gap measures" (see *SCIR*, pp. 350–358), the savings bank is not even in the same gap, and yet is "caused by" the gap. If the process of differentiation is not strongly tied together in its different parts, then it cannot be formally adequate as an explanatory scheme.

## THE PROBLEMS OF RUNNING A FAMILY

Our Bolton spinner worrying about wildish children, out of control of the only adults who could be trusted to discipline and train them, the child's parents, is pointing to a real problem. One can easily imagine other spinners worrying about how to raise their children when they work 14 hours a day and the children are elsewhere. What had made the factory a reasonable place to raise children was the fact that they were under their parents' supervision in the factory. Now we consider a capitalist installing new machines that need more assistants (normally children and adolescents), and a child labor bill that takes the children away from the factory (and consequently from the parents) for at least a large part of the day. Neither the capitalist nor the legislator is likely to be very worried about a spinner's problem supervising his children.

If we find that new machinery and factory work had been easily accepted as long as family groups worked the machines, but sudden signs of great excitement when the machines "require" more children and fewer adults, and when children have to have a different schedule, that suggests that the excitement is connected with the disruption of family functions, not with either machinery or factories. This excitement has components of sober realistic analysis of the problem, (like that of the Bolton spinner), strikes against new machinery, accusations of heartlessness of masters, utopian visions of a 10-hour day or of reconstruction of society along new lines, and the like.

The sober analysis convinces us that the problem might be where Smelser says it is; the visions of doom and revolutionary reconstruction along cooperative lines both show that the workers were taking *something* very seriously. The fact that all kinds of excitement ebbed after children were unequivocally decided not to belong in the factory, but instead in a (reconstructed) home to which the father came after a reduced working day, also supports the causal argument. The fact that after this time, all sorts of provisions for apprenticeship in the factory declined, and several sorts of schooling outside the factory grew, also suggests that the disappearance of family preparation for adulthood from the factory provided fertile conditions for the growth of other methods of training.

That is, what renders the account convincing is (a) evidence of continuity of family authority in work in early spinning factories up to around 1830; (b) evidence that no one worried about family authority in spinning factories after around 1840; (c) evidence that family authority in the factory was undermined by specific new machines and specific legislation; and (d) evidence that workers were very worried about the problems this brought up for them.

If the evidence brought to bear on the general scheme of interpretation is not convincing, the evidence for the broad proposition that many of the troubles of industrialization are caused by family disruption is convincing. The crucial point in the argument is that the most extreme collective behavior of *spinners* did not occur until the period 1820–1840, while factory labor in spinning had been introduced by around 1800. The argument is that only mule spinning, introduced on a large scale after the Napoleonic wars, disrupted spinners' families.

> It will be recalled that the effects of the larger mules with more spindles in the 1820's were (1) to reduce spinners' piece-rates on the larger machines; (2) to increase spinners' weekly wages on these machines; (3) to threaten some technological unemployment, at least in the short run; (4) to increase the physical exertion of labourers on the larger machines; (5) to increase the number of assistants per spinner; and (6) to endanger the apprenticeship system based on kinship, and thus to undermine the economic authority of the spinner. Almost all the social turbulence which engulfed the factory operatives in the 1820's and 1830's reflects an attempt to minimize these effects and to restore the traditional ways [*SCIR*, p. 231].

It is the last two of these difficulties that Smelser particularly emphasizes as sources of the "disturbed" or "utopian" agitations of the 1820s and 1830s, difficulties eventually resolved by the reorganization of the family and work roles of children and by the limitation of factory hours.

His attempt to support this argument has two main parts. One of these has to do with showing that the realtion of family to work was different in three different situations: (a) spinning in factories before 1820; (b) spinning in factories after 1820; and (c) in hand-loom weaving throughout the period after 1806, and especially after 1816. The second tries to establish that these differences in family–work relations explain (a) the time pattern of spinners' participation in utopian and reform activity (after 1820, but dying out with the 10-hours bill); (b) the differences in such participation between factory operatives (especially spinners) and hand-loom weavers (weavers consistently more extreme); and (c) the content of working class agitation, especially the content of its "utopian" and "fantasy" symbols during periods of greatest excitement.

The overall strategy of the argument and the mobilization of evidence for it is very closely related to the general scheme of Smelser's (and Parsons') laws of differentiation, a general scheme I have rejected above. My purpose here will be to argue that Smelser was led to correct analyses of historical data by exactly the same scheme that led him to make the sorts of mistakes already outlined. If this argument is accepted, then the problem is to sort out the methodological virtues of the work from the penumbra of bad theory that caused those virtues.

Briefly, my argument will be that three kinds of exploration of similarities between historical situations guided the valuable part of the analysis. The first is the comparison of middle points in a temporal development (e.g., factory spinning before 1820) with ideal type descriptions of the beginning points (e.g., spinning by wives and children in weavers' homes) and ending points (spinning by full-time employees in factories, whose wives and children, if any, spend much of their time at home or in school). The second is a comparison of the historical development of different sorts of changes (e.g., spinning factory operative versus domestic hand-loom weaver). These comparisons involve both the causal variables (e.g., pressures causing family disruption) and the effect variables (e.g., agitation with overtones of moralistic despair). The final type of argument depends on a comparison of functional equivalents in the states before and after the transformation.

For the first of these, I will adopt the name *ideal sequence comparison*. The logic behind it is relatively simple, but the methodological guidelines it produces are unfortunately quite complex, and a really descriptive name would be at least a paragraph long. For the second, I will adopt the name *comparative histories of roles*; for the third, *argument from functional completeness*.


## IDEAL SEQUENCE COMPARISON

The logic of "ideal sequence comparison" rests on the logic of "historically specific functionalism," that systems can meet their functional prerequisites only under historically limited circumstances. What we start with are two functioning systems, a beginning system and an ending system, that appear to be reasonably stable resolutions of a continuing dilemma of social organization, such as how to relate the family and work. One way to relate the family and work is the putting out system, in which some part of the total production process (e.g., spinning and weaving) is allocated to a number of families who specialize in that process (weaving families), who then use family institutions to organize the production work (e.g., use the father's authority to organize the work of children) and also simultaneously use the production work to satisfy the requirements of the family (money in the first instance, but also training children for a useful occupation). This system, in fact, occurred historically as a dominant way to organize the production of cloth, lasted quite a long while as a dominant system, and did not, during that period, produce such severe internal contradictions as to destroy it. At a specific period in history, before about 1790 in England, then, this system "met its functional requirements" and was "functional" under those conditions.

Another system that also met its own requirements under different circumstances (after 1840) was a system in which male adults and young women worked in spinning factories (sometimes with factory power-loom weaving), married women took care of the home and children, and children were trained (in part) by schools.

These two systems are related to each other partly by both being located in Lancashire in the cotton industry some 50 years apart, but more fundamentally by being functional substitutes for each other. That is, if the later system exists, the previous one is replaced, competed out of existence by the "more differentiated" structure of factory labor and separate home and educational institutions. Thus, a historical analysis of the shift from one to the other has to be an analysis of functional equivalence and structural superiority of the second system.

What we extract from these two historically functional systems, then, is a list of contrasts. This list in this case might include:

| *Putting out (before 1790)* | *Factory (after 1840)* |
|---|---|
| Family authority over subordinates | Officials appointed by master of factory |
| Family owns capital equipment | Master owns equipment |
| Merchant capitalist owns goods in process | Productive capitalist owns goods in process |
| Children trained by father during work | Children trained by school |
| Married women work at home in production | Married women are housewives |
| Father governs division between productive work and leisure, family responsibilities | Work hours determined by law |

It is important to note that these contrasts are, by hypothesis, parts of two integrated functional systems. Both systems produce cotton; both produce children ready to enter the productive system. These are, then, not just any old ideal types, but ideal types that satisfy the requirements of their own (historically limited) continuity. Further, the beginning ideal type turned into the ending ideal type in a period of about 50 years, in the sense that one system was dominant before 1790 and the other dominant after 1840. That must mean that, somehow or other, the old system lost viability in that period, while the new system gained a competitive advantage. But the new system had to be built, and it took around 50 years to do it, 50 years full of strife, collective agitation, Owenism, Cobbettism, Chartism, Cooperation, Methodism, and other outbursts of social and moral sentiments. This, then, is the basic structure of the explanatory problem.

The next step is to specify the intermediate steps by describing the analogies at each major point with the beginning and end points. For example, in the spinning part of the process, there were three major stages: the improvement of spinning in the home by use of the small jenny and mule; the movement of spinning from the home to the factory with the invention of the water-frame mule and larger jennies around 1800; and then the undermining of family authority within the factory by the increase in the size of mules in the 1820s.

Stage 1:

From the standpoint of social structure, however, the cottage jenny and mule reshuffled rather than reorganized labour. The main earning power, at least after 1780, still rested with the husband, whether spinner or weaver. Some women began to weave beside their husbands, but in other cases the wife became more secondary economically because hand-spinning had been taken from her. Further, the new cottage machines did not disturb the traditional relationship between father and son; in either spinning or weaving the father continued to instruct his son in the trade. Perhaps more important, the other family functions of child-rearing and tension-management were relatively unaltered, because the family economy remained in the home. In many ways, therefore, the period between 1780 and 1790 was a "golden age" for the domestic spinner; his earnings increased, but the structure of his employment remained the same [SCIR, pp. 184–185].

Stage 2:

Side by side with the domestic jenny and mule came the water-frame and the mill. While we should not minimize the hardships in these early mills, particularly for parish apprentices, we must remember the correctives which preserved many features of the traditional family. A clear example was the practice of hiring whole families in the country mills. In general the proportion of adult males was low; perhaps they amounted to only one in ten employees at a typical mill in the 1780's or 1790's. Masters often hired the head of the family, however, for road-making, bridge-building, or plant construction while employing the wife and children in the mill. Such an arrangement not only augmented the family income, but also allowed for the presence of a parent with the children during working hours [SCIR, p. 185].

The only available information on the industry's age–sex composition in these years shows that adult males constituted only 17.7% of the total employees listed in parliamentary returns in 1816, while for six mills in Nottinghamshire the figure was 18.54%.

All these trends threatened to disperse the family through the factories at the cost of its tradition and solidarity. The recruitment of women and children weakened the traditional domestic basis for child-rearing. Because the opportunities for the adult male in the industry were limited, his status as chief breadwinner in the family was in danger. Furthermore, it was becoming harder for him to train his children for a trade, particularly as the domestic spinning machinery became progressively less competitive [SCIR, p. 188].

Clearly the interests of the family invaded the recruitment of child labour. Witnesses before the parliamentary committees from 1816 through 1819 testified consistently that masters allowed the operative spinners to hire their own assistants (piecers, scavengers, etc.) and that the spinners chose their wives, children, near relatives, or relatives of the proprietors. Many children, especially the youngest, entered the mill at the express request of their parents. One manager claimed that children under ten either were employed by their own parents or were the children of widows. Finally, most of the early trade unions' rules explicitly prohibited members from recruiting assistants outside the narrowly defined classes of children, brothers, orphan nephews, etc.

In the early 1820's, therefore, a child entered the factory at the age of eight or nine years as a scavenger who worked for his father; he cleaned machinery, gathered waste cotton, etc. If designated for future spinning he became a piecer, mending broken threads for a number of years. He was trained to spin until seventeen or eighteen when he finally became a spinner. If destined for the cardroom, he was transferred there after several years of scavenging [SCIR, pp. 188–189].

In 1792 and again in 1795 the Friendly Associated Cotton Spinners of Manchester prohibited spinners from teaching anybody to spin except their own children or paupers who were in receipt of parish relief. Others were forced to pay the high price of £1 1s. The stockport mule-spinners in 1795 and the Oldham spinners in 1796 made the same prohibitions. See Articles, Rules, Orders and Regulations . . . of the Friendly Associated Cotton Spinners . . . of Manchester (Manchester, 1792 and 1795), Article XVI in the 1792 Rules and Article XV in the 1795 Rules; Articles, Rules, Orders and Regulations of the Friendly Associated Mule Cotton Spinners . . . of Stockport (Stockport, 1795), p. 12; for the Oldham rules, cf. Webb Manuscripts on Trade Unionism, Vol. VII, p. 171. In the resolutions of the delegate meeting of the Operative Spinners of England, Ireland and Scotland drawn up in 1829, the restrictions specified only the son, brother, or orphan nephews of operatives, or poor relations of proprietors. Reprinted in Webb Manuscripts on Trade Unionism, Vol. XXXIV, p. 31. The Association of Operative Cotton Spinners of Glasgow and Neighbourhood were reported in 1838 to restrict training to sons and brothers of members. Parliamentary Papers, 1837–8, VII, Combinations of Workmen, p. 303–6 [SCIR, p. 189].

## Stage 3:

To increase the number of assistants per spinner. In 1819 a Manchester spinner testified that for 504 spindles (on two mules) he required two piecers, his wife and brother. In 1832 another spinner estimated that three children would be employed to assist one adult in fine spinning. The following year an example of four assistants per spinner was given for a hypothetical factory. Also in 1833 a factory commissioner produced an even more extreme estimate after conversations with persons in the trade. By his estimates the improved mules would change the ratio of assistants to adult spinners from 4:1 to 9:1. While these estimates cannot be taken literally, it is clear that such alterations would distort the relative proportions of spinners and assistants [SCIR, pp. 197–198].

In 1838 a Glasgow lawyer affirmed that the restrictions of piecers to sons or brothers "has never been acted upon; they (the spinners) found it impossible to do so; and at this moment I have ascertained, from minute inquiry, there are no less than 1,305 children of hand-loom weavers employed as piecers to 950 spinners in Glasgow and its vicinity at this moment, so that (the Cotton Spinners' Association in Glasgow) is not of (an) exclusive character."

The last two effects were particularly important from the standpoint of the differentiation of the family's economic roles. Because the semi-apprenticeship system based on kinship was on the wane, it was becoming more difficult to maintain that fusion between the economic authority of the parent and other socialization functions [SCIR, p. 199].

I have supplied more quotations for Stage 2 because the critical point in Smelser's argument is that many of the features of the *old working-class family system* were preserved for some 20 years *inside the spinning factory*. That is, we can break up the process of moving from the beginning point into two major reorganizations: the movement of *spinning families* into the factory, producing a temporary equilibrium from about 1800 to 1820; then *the breakup of spinning families within the factory* from 1820 to 1840, finally resulting in a new equilibrium state after the 10-hours bill. The argument is, then, that those social movements that had to do with uncertainties of family arrangements among spinners were *not* produced by the spinning factory, but *were* produced by the destruction of family arrangements within the factory.

If this argument is true, then Smelser has to show that the frequency and the character of collective disturbances in which spinners participated changed in a way that corresponded to these partial shifts. At the early stage, where the problem is starting to move spinning from the domestic putting-out system into factories, we have the following description:

> The wholesale destruction of machinery in Lancashire in 1779 reflects both influences. The new jennies, water-frames, and carding-engines seemed to imperil the livelihood of the domestic hand-workers. For years, furthermore, the American Revolutionary War had tightened economic conditions in the trade. Destruction began with an attack upon the "larger factories and more prosperous concerns," and within a few days mobs had destroyed much printing machinery and either smashed large jennies or pared them down to twenty spindles. The symbolism is interesting for the mobs attacked machinery only of factory size; cottage machines were acceptable because they had not altered the traditional arrangements of production radically. Shortly after the attacks, workers claimed in a petition that old stock cards and smaller jennies could supply the necessary quantity of high-quality work. Several years later a petition from Leicester complained of technological unemployment, and cited the advantages of the domestic system for training children and attending the sick and aged.
> According to the Hammonds, "after these riots in 1779 the workers made no more attempts to check the introduction of machinery for spinning" [*SCIR*, p. 228].

During the period of temporary equilibrium with the spinning family in the factory, Smelser argues:

> Most disputes dealt with wage-levels, though occasionally the question of filling work vacancies arose. Most violence was directed not against machinery but against "knobsticks" (scabs) whom masters employed to break strikes. Most strikes, furthermore, occurred in good times when spinners desired a share of the prosperity and when their striking power was enhanced by the temporary shortage of labour [*SCIR*, p. 229].

But during the period of pressure on the family we find a union official talking about wild interesting women:

> Girls, many of them interesting ones, from 14 to 20 years of age, are thus rendered independent of their natural guardians, who in many cases, indeed, become in consequence of this very employment, dependent upon their children. In this unnatural and unwholesome state of things, the reins of government are broken, and the excited feelings of youth and inexperience let loose upon the world, a prey too often to pride, vice, and infamy [*SCIR*, p. 232].

And a former Bolton spinner worrying about wild children before they get interesting (see the quotation about boys and girls of a wildish nature). And protests about the inequality of piece rates even though workers on the new machines made more money:

> Strikes to resist superior machinery began clearly in 1823 when "spinners" (in Bolton) complain of reductions in the prices paid on large wheels "when they have to keep more piecers and work harder themselves." Two years earlier a strike had broken out when masters had submitted a new list of prices. Both these Bolton strikes failed. In 1824 a larger strike developed in Hyde when spinners claimed they made only 3s. 7d. per 1,000 of No. 40's, whereas other spinners made 4s. 7d. On their improved machinery, however, these Hyde spinners were earning higher weekly wages than others. In the following year, one of the precipitating factors in a strike in Chorley was the possibility of reduced prices on the larger wheels. The years 1825–6 brought depression and "lack of cohesion and concerted action amongst the workers." One strike with violence, however broke out in Oldham after several mills introduced new prices [SCIR, p. 233].

And participation in a wide variety of social movements with somewhat contradictory visions of society:

> Many a northern operative professed to be a trade unionist, a radical, an Owenite co-operator, and a Ten Hours man all at the same time, actively serving (like John Doherty) in all four movements. There was thus a bewildering tendency for the various organizations to fade into one another; sometimes to vanish altogether and then reappear in another guise [SCIR, p. 239].

Further, the specific demands of the operatives were of a kind that attempted to preserve families working together, for instance by urging that their own hours be reduced to those of the children after the law of 1833:

> The success of the movement interests us less than the fact that the operatives turned at this time to an obviously impractical demand, shrouded in symptoms of disturbance, for exactly eight hours. The movement followed a long period of costly and unsuccessful strikes as well as the recent indifference and hostility to the operatives' entreaties for a ten-hour day. Furthermore, eight hours coincided with the number of hours which Parliament had recently established for children between nine and thirteen. One element in the abortive scheme for national regeneration, therefore, was to re-link the labour of adult and child, thus returning to a less differentiated family organization [SCIR, p. 243].

and then for extending the hours of children to equal those of adults:

> The characteristics of the operatives' activities during the next three years lend support to this interpretation. In late 1835 "in one town after another" gatherings of operatives voted by "a large majority" to press for a twelve-hour day for children, a figure coinciding with the average number of hours worked by adults. Many operatives were prepared to extend the labor of children, even though they had complained bitterly years before of the moral and physical distresses imposed by long hours [SCIR, p. 243].

Finally, and to Smelser most persuasive, the imagery of many of these movements was a peculiar combination of utopian and reactionary

> And to begin a system of education to teach men industrial skills and women to "wash, bake, brew, make and mend clothes and stockings; all in all other duties appertaining to Cottage Economy." The Society's literature refers repeatedly to co-operative notions such as the labour theory of value, the attack upon machine-owners who rob labourers of their fair share of this value, etc. There were also attacks upon "the fund-holder, dead weight men, army and navy men, jew, and capitalist." Scapegoating and utopian idealization of the past were in clear evidence [SCIR, p. 242].

> The social ideology of Cobbettism idealized the division of family labour of the recent past. Cobbett visualized an independent yeoman or craftsman at the head of the family and a wife who rose early, worked hard, reared her children, baked and brewed. What prevented this Utopia was the whole commercial and industrial system—interest, paper money, money-lenders, Jews, rich and crude factory-owners, and sinecures. Cobbett felt, furthermore, that radical reform of representation in Parliament would effect a miraculous achievement of this Utopia [SCIR, p. 250].

Notes of good sense so pervade this "utopian" literature, and the utopian capitalist rhetoric of the opponents or of conservatives is so similar (except that the utopian capitalists won), that it is hard to sort out the evidence on this. For example, compare the good sense of the quotation given above about how new machines doing the work of 10 men benefit the master, not the workman, with the explicit denial of the reality of some kinds of evidence by the representatives of social control.

> Furthermore, when the Commission entered Manchester on its business, the ten hour agitators prepared a giant demonstration similar to that which had greeted Sadler's committee one year earlier. The Commission indicated, in a chilly manner, that it was not to be influenced by such demonstrations of public opinion as appeals from children in person [SCIR, p. 292].

And the casual sacrifice of an important English value (the welfare of children) to another English value more convenient for employers:

Children's hours alone might be reduced because children were not free agents and hence were outside the scope of the value of independence. For adult labour, however, the Commission was forced to weigh two traditional elements in conflict: (a) the independence of adult labour, deeply rooted in the value-system of the day; (b) the traditional economic relationship between parent and child, deeply rooted in the social structure of the operative class. In choosing to sacrifice the latter to the former, the Commission exemplifies still another line of "channelling"—to reaffirm the value-system, and to rule out lines of action (such as universal ten hour labour) which might threaten its integrity [SCIR, pp. 291–292].

*Integrity* is surely a heavy word. In the value system of capitalists being defended here, money surely plays a role alongside integrity of values.

The point that is supposed to be demonstrated by these pieces of evidence is that the agitation changed from being about wages to being objection to the structural reorganization of factory work which undermined family life in the mills.

> These structural strikes, in my opinion, represented the operatives' attempt to resist the pressures of the improved machinery on the family division of labour—pressures to modify the traditional wage-structure, to multiply the number of assistants, to throw heads of families out of employment, and to hasten the general deterioration of the spinners' authority. The operatives' interest was to maintain these more generalized elements of the family economy. The stikes alone, however, do not exhaust the evidence regarding such disturbances [SCIR, p. 235].

Even though some of the qualitative analysis of the content of agitation is perhaps too eager, the general logic is straightforward. The detailed analogy of family life in the spinning factories to pre-factory life, and its disruption between 1820 and 1840, establishes the timing and social location of the causal variable. The attempt to demonstrate that spinners' agitation after 1820 had new elements, elements closely connected with the family and with symbols of ideal family life, is an attempt to separate the effects of the gross changes of industrialization from the effects of specific changes in family organization within the factory.

## COMPARATIVE HISTORIES OF ROLES

This argument is supplemented by a strategic comparison of factory operatives (specifically, male spinners) with hand-loom weavers. At the time (before electricity), power looms had to be located in factories, while hand looms could be located in cottages. But the crucial difference in the technical situation was that only after many small improvements did a power loom become as much as 20% more efficient than a hand loom (see *SCIR*, pp. 149 and 156), while large spinning machines were from the first enormously more productive than spinning wheels (in 1830 hand spinning in India cost about five times as much as power spinning on self-acting mules in England [*SCIR*, p. 127]). That is, technical and economic pressures moved spinning to factories very fast, while a hand loom was still a close, if poor, competitor to a power loom in the 1830s.

The overall result of this technical near-competitiveness of hand looms was a double development: the preservation of cottage industry in hand-loom weaving in a progressively worsening economic situation and the organization of factories on a nonfamily basis, employing women and youths. The long-term result of the poor competitive situation was an absolute decline in weavers' wages, and an even more marked decline by comparison with rising factory wages.

> We have seen that the first response of the weavers was to encourage females to weave in greater numbers and to apprentice children at an early age. Weavers' children also began to enter the factories in increasing numbers. In 1818 a witness attributed both early apprenticeship and children in factories to the low wages of weaving "of late years." The figures in Appendix B show a liberal number of weavers' children in the Catrine Works. Certainly the economic if not the social conditions of the factory encouraged child labour. Even "little children" could make more money in the factory than the father could earn on the loom. In 1824 a man and wife together could earn 10s. or 11s. on the hand-loom, but a child of fifteen years could earn 7s. in the factory, and one of ten years could earn 6s., which together would exceed their parents' earnings. Already the father's status as breadwinner was being undermined [*SCIR*, p. 206].

Thus, while the advent of spinning machinery both boosted the cottage industry of weaving (by supplying plentiful and competitively priced raw materials) and moved spinning families into the factory, the advent of the power loom undermined the family in the cottage and gave it no place to go (except as individuals, especially children) in the factory.

> The extinction of the adult male weaver displaced the economic head of the household and thus reorganized the occupational structure much more dramatically [*SCIR*, p. 245].

> The major difference was that, in weaving, the recruitment of young persons

and children fell into the hands of the masters, not the operatives. In 1834 Samuel Stanway analysed returns from 151 Lancashire cotton mills. In spinning the operatives still recruited most employees under eighteen, despite the inroads on their authority. Of 6,599 male employees under eighteen in spinning, operatives hired 5,852 and masters only 697 (50 employees unclassifiable). For females under eighteen, operatives hired 2,284 out of 2,654 and masters only 346 (24 unclassifiable). In weaving, on the other hand, the masters' recruitment predominated. Of 1,631 males under eighteen, masters hired 986 and operatives 610 (35 unclassifiable). Of 3,674 females under eighteen, masters hired 2,538 and the operatives only 1,104 (32 unclassifiable). With the introduction of the power-loom, the recruitment of young labour undoubtedly began to supersede those kinship and community ties which had operated so strongly in the spinning branches [SCIR, pp. 200–201].

Further, this attack on family integrity was a long-run evolution, forced by a small competitive advantage that could be met temporarily by reducing the labor income of weaving families.

If this argument applies to weavers, then, they should have been under intense pressure, both economic pressure and pressure to reorganize the family to get at least the children out of the disastrous situation. Thus in contrast to (spinning) factory operatives, weavers should have been (a) more continuously radical and utopian, not having distinct stages before 1820 and after, and (b) more desperate, more violent, more utopian, more inclined to use family–utopian symbols. This argument is made in detail in Smelser's book (cf. pp. 245–264). An example on the participation in the meeting leading to the massacre at Peterloo:

Of the 69 traceable signatures on the requisition for the Peterloo meeting, 46 were weavers; of the 200 killed and injured whose occupations are listed, 150 were weavers. Read "The Social and Economic Background to Peterloo," op. cit., p. 16 [SCIR, p. 252].

## THE ARGUMENT FROM FUNCTIONAL COMPLETENESS

If it is true that much of working-class agitation during this period was due to pressures to reorganize family roles, then its overall content ought to have been shaped by the functional requirements of a complete family system. That is, if both the beginning point and the end point have to be functionally viable family systems, and if the traditional family-working-together structure that met those requirements was being undermined, there ought to have been pressure to invent new institutions for those functions.

Thus one can solidify the argument if one can show any of three phenomena during this same period: (*a*) that institutions outside the factory or putting-out system were invented and developed during this same period to serve functions previously served by the family-working-together; (*b*) that those parts of the population under most pressure for family reorganization disproportionately used these institutions to fulfill these family functions; and (*c*) that the effective functioning of these institutions produced satisfaction with newly organized family life, or at least that it decreased agitation with family themes.

Several institutions are analyzed wholly or partly from this point of view by Smelser: Methodism and Nonconformism,[2] the Ten Hour Bill, trade unions, small depositor savings banks. In many ways, the most convincing of these arguments is the one on the Ten Hours Bill, so let us summarize that argument briefly.

Factory legislation before the Ten Hours Bill (specifically the Factory Act of 1833) had regulated the work of children and young people, and had helped to undermine the spinning family in the factory. It did this by limiting children's hours to a smaller number than adult hours (adult hours were implicitly regulated to 12 hours a day by limiting adolescents to 12 hours), and by requiring schooling to be given to working children. This tended to push children out of the factory.

From data on the Catrine Cotton Works, Smelser argues:

Hence the following rank, based on the probable wages of the head of the family:

| Rank | Category | Percentage of children of all ages employed |
|------|----------|:---:|
| 1 | Males in mill | 61.8 |
| 2 | "Others" | 66.6 |
| 3 | Weavers | 76.3 |
| 4 | Widows in mill | 77.1 |
| 5 | Widows not in mill | 85.3 |

It is plausible to assume from these figures that families reaching a more differentiated role in the labour force as factory operatives (spinners, dressers, mechanics, overlookers, etc.) were also working their children less in general. Part of this effect is enforced by the fact of differentiation itself; if the economic role of the adult splits from the child, the processes of socialization probably were transferred more to the home. Another contributing factor was of course the wage-level. For adults whose factory employment meant a higher income,

[2]Actually this is treated more as a cause of industrialization, as influencing values, than as a functional substitute for moral training in the family, except when it comes to Sunday schools. A little less Weber and a little more examinations of the functions of the congregation in working class life would have improved the argument.

to employ children was no longer so necessary; they could afford the luxury of differentiation. On the other hand, those in economically precarious positions, either because of special circumstances (e.g., widows) or because of long-term pressures (e.g., weavers), were forced to send their children into the factories [*SCIR*, p. 223].

After the Ten Hours Bill was passed, an interview study of factory operatives *whose wages had been reduced by reduced hours* (other operatives were eliminated) overwhelmingly endorsed the reduced hours (almost two to one—see *SCIR*, p. 305).

Of the men, 82¾% preferred either ten or eleven hours, as opposed to 63⅓% of the women. Wage-levels also influenced the preferences.

In an attempt to shed more light on these responses and on our interpretive scheme, I calculated in the Appendix the distribution of responses of men and women according to (a) marital and parental status and (b) their wage-level. While all the results are not significant statistically, the following patterns of preference appeared among the operatives:

| Prefer 10 hours | Prefer more than 10 hours |
|---|---|
| Unmarried men | Married men |
| Men earning more than 17s. 6d. weekly | Men earning 17s. 6d. or less weekly |
| Married men earning more than 17s. 6d. weekly | Married men earning 17s. 6d. or less weekly |
| Men with 0 or 1 children | Men with 2 or more children |
| Men with 0 or 1 children earning more than 17s. 6d. weekly | Men with 0 or 1 children earning 17s. 6d. or less weekly |
| Men with 2 or more children earning more than 17s. 6d. weekly | Men with 2 or more children earning 17s. 6d. or less weekly |
| Married women | Unmarried women |
| Women earning more than 8s. weekly | Women earning 8s. or less weekly |
| Married women earning more than 8s. weekly | Married women earning 8s. or less weekly |
| Women with children earning more than 8s. weekly | Women with children earning 8s. or less weekly |
| Childless married women earning more than 8s. weekly | Childless married women earning 8s. or less weekly [*SCIR*, p. 306]. |

That is, male operatives *both* kept their children out of the mills more *and* preferred to work only 10 hours, even at lower wages. Smelser's argument then is that if one builds his family outside the mill, and wants to have any time to be with them (and can afford the new kind of family), he needs to have time off from work. The new factory legislation was in part the product of agitation that Smelser has attributed to the family troubles of exactly those people (male spinners) who most quickly adopt the new kind of family, and are most enthusiastic about the bill that lets them have some time with that new family. The leisure, then, is a functional substitute for supervision of one's children in the factory. Those who most need the substitute (by the argument about spinners' problems in the 1820s) are those who most use it.

## THE THEORY AND THE STRATEGY

Clearly the evidence Smelser gives is about the same subject as his theory, the differentiation of a functional system. Clearly, also, the explanatory principle to which the evidence speaks is Smelser's, that pressures to divide the role of family-as-producer into the two roles of factory operative and household-functioning-outside-the-factory produced many of the features of working-class agitation from 1800 to 1840. Clearly, the functional components of the beginning system and the ending system were suggested to Smelser by the Parsonian 16-fold scheme which gives four functional aspects to the economy and four interrelated ones to the family. And finally, the evidence already presented, particularly on spinners, is a stage process of uneven developments over time, somewhat like the seven-stage process in his theory. In short, Smelser would have been unlikely to write the monograph he did without the theory.

But consider the difference between the stage of "spinning family in the factory" and that of "encouragement of the resulting proliferation of new ideas, without imposing specific responsibility for their implementation or for 'taking the consequences' [SCIR, p. 40]." The second of these is, as Smelser puts it, a "theoretical box," perhaps one we might find in this world. The first is a typification of a social system that exists in this world, for instance in Manchester between 1800 and 1820. It is specifically differentiated from what existed before (spinning and weaving families in a putting-out system) and from what came after (factories with individual rather than family labor contracts). It has an inner causal coherence, by the contraint that if it does not meet its functional requirements it disappears (as it eventually did in fact).

If we were to look responsibly for a "new irresponsible ideas" stage, we would have to describe it as a social system. Such a stage needs people trained and motivated to produce irresponsible ideas, needs experimental workshops or libraries or other facilities, needs principles of justice in the reward system for ideas, needs goals and a system for determining authoritatively what sorts of ideas would be valuable. In short, it needs to meet its functional requirements. And if it were going to be replaced by a stage of entrepreneurship, of responsibly implementing new ideas, its functional requirements would have to be undermined and the requirements of entrepreneurship would have to come into historical existence.

That is, the problem of establishing the seven stages of differentiation is precisely the same sort of enterprise as that of establishing that spinning factories first reorganized capital without reorganizing family labor, then only later reorganized family labor. The strategies of "ideal sequence comparison," "comparative histories of roles," and "argument from functional completeness" would therefore bear on the question of a stage of irresponsible ideas just as they do on the question of a stage of family-in-the-factory. For in order to exist in and disappear from this world, such a stage must be shown to meet its own requirements for a while, then not to meet them.

Smelser's success (or at least relative success) in analyzing the stages in the growth of a modern factory worker's role, and his lack of success in finding seven stages of the social differentiation process, thus rest on applying or not applying a strategy for classifying historical facts together or distinguishing them from each other. This strategy has several critical components.

1. The explanatory problem is set by noting a deep analogy between two social systems that occur at historically separated times. The analogy between the putting-out spinning and weaving family and the factory worker with a household outside the factory is one of "fulfilling the same set of functions." Clearly this analogy is informed by general functional theory; but it is also constructed out of the concrete historical materials.

2. Particular intervening structures are then distinguished from each other, according to the similarities and differences in the way some of these functions get performed. Particularly strategic comparisons are those that make earlier stages somewhat similar to the beginning, (e.g., the spinning family in the factory) and later stages somewhat similar to the end (e.g., the large double-decked self-acting mule with a large number of helpers for each spinner).

3. Roles are distinguished from one another by the character of the intervening stages (e.g., spinners versus hand loom cottage weav-

ers), especially by *which* functions are handled in a new way (power loom labor force recruited by masters rather than by heads of families), and whether the role is advantaged or undermined by the developing system.

4. General social structures (such as factory legislation, trade unions, savings banks) are distinguished by whether or not they serve functions that need substitute structures in the new order, and by evidence that the people who supposedly newly need such structures show differential use of and enthusiasm for them.

The network of historical analogies in the argument is a network of functional equivalence. But empty boxes of functions that maybe ought to be performed (such as encouraging irresponsible ideas) are quite often hard to fill, both for the theorist and for people like the desperate hand loom weavers, who encouraged Owenite ideas so irresponsible that Smelser calls them disturbed.

That is, when Smelser uses his theory to construct detailed analogies and differences between functioning systems, the theory works. When he uses it to find a few facts that fit an abstract theoretical scheme, it does not work.

## BENDIX ON MANAGEMENT IDEOLOGY

The overall intellectual purpose of Bendix's *Work and Authority in Industry* is to explore the historical sources of a "pluralist" rather a "totalitarian" resolution of the problems of labor relations. This is clearly part of a larger interest in the social sources of political freedom, which Bendix believes must be investigated historically. I believe that the problem of the social supports of political freedom is a central problem of any humane social science, that variations in labor relations are a central cause of variations in political freedom, and that labor relations systems must be studied historically. I am not, however, going to address these larger linkages of his monograph—to sociological theory and to humane concerns—here. Consequently, I am not going to analyze the central methodology that is designed to address those questions, the set of parellel contrasts between nineteenth-century England and Russia and between twentieth-century America and East Germany.

What I will try to do instead is to examine the methodology of one of the country studies, that of England. The overall comparison between countries gets much of its power from the residue of the reader's feelings of satisfaction with the historical–causal analysis within each country. That is, it is because we are satisfied that through Methodism, through appeals to working-class ambition, through the Anti-Corn Law League's

agitation, the entrepreneurs in England appealed to the workers and
ended up addressing them as fellow citizens, that we are easily per-
suaded that Russian entrepreneurs' appeals to government officials
for more repression might have a very different long-run effect
on the citizenship of workers. Bendix's causal analysis goes forward
at two levels, one within countries and one comparative. If we ask
why the comparative parts have a ring of reality to them, while
hundreds of cross tabulations of levels of development against
levels of totalitarianism leave us theoretically impoverished, we must
answer in terms of the richness of support for the overall inferences
in the within-country analysis. The within-country analysis is much less
explicitly justified by Bendix on a theoretical level, and for that reason
I will concentrate on it here.

What I will be trying to do, then, is much the same logically as I tried
to do in the analysis of Smelser—to show that the impression of theoretical solidity does not (or does not mainly) come from the formal theoretical apparatus. It comes, rather, from the theory built up in the analysis
of historical sequences, by specifying in considerable detail how instances in that history are either analogous or different.

Roughly speaking, the overall argument in each historical section of
Bendix's book has the following structure. The entrepreneurs or managers have some sort of problem in advancing their own interests which
requires support from some other social group. For example, a defense
of the worthwhileness of entrepreneurical activity may be directed toward an aristocracy that controls symbols of social honor. The nature of
that appeal is determined by what the entrepreneurs or managers want
out of the other group, the historical situation in which they have to seek
it, and by the nature of the group appealed to. In the course of this
appeal, strategic choices are made about how to conceive both the group
appealed to, and other groups involved in the situation (e.g., conceptions of the workers in factories may become involved because aristocratic politicans accuse the bourgeoisie of exploitation). These embedded
conceptions of the moral nature, the role, the possibilities of development, of social groups become a deposit in the civic culture of the community and shape the next steps of ideological evolution. For example, if
entrepreneurs claim social honor in competition with aristocrats because
of manly devotion to production in contrast to unproductive aristocratic
heirs, this leaves a deposit in their conceptions of the bourgeoisie and its
role, and shapes the nature of their defense of superior status over
workers in succeeding periods.

The key to the causal unity of an ideological campaign, then, is a
combination of a problem which requires an appeal and a collective
ideological strategy for resolving that problem. The problem itself has

several components: What do the entrepreneurs or managers lack that some other group (at least partly) controls; what is the conception the *other* group itself has of its role in the situation; what is the previous historical deposit of conceptions of the moral qualities and possibilities of development of the groups involved in the problem; on what basis can the entrepreneurs and managers themselves be unified—how much diversity among interests can be unified by concentration on a particular problem and a particular ideological strategy for dealing with it?

Bendix believes that some kinds of ideological problems are common to all authorities, some common to all industrializing elites or all managers of modern large-scale enterprises, and some distinctive of particular historical situations. This last fact is one of the reasons a historical analysis is necessary.

But even within a given historical situation, it is problematic *whether any ideology* will unify entrepreneurs and managers, and *what the content* of that ideology will be. In broadly similar circumstances of competition for honor and privilege with an aristocracy, some entrepreneurs may invent and be loyal to an Anti–Corn Law League that attacks aristocratic economic privileges in alliance with workers, while others join the Tories to associate themselves with the aristocracy or to preserve social peace against working class agitation. The historical deposit of a conception of workers' roles in a civic culture depends not only on the entrepreneurical problem but also on the "historical accidents" that determine which kind of resolution of that problem leaves the deposit. Because the relation of the entrepreneurs' problem and its ideological solution is not determinate, one needs to add historical specificity to describe the nature of the ideological deposit.

To put it another way, the existence of a historical problem of a given type—for instance, defending entrepreneurial authority in a political system dominated by aristocrats—is an explanation of a *tendency to ideologize*. But such tendencies to ideologize can be capitalized into social movements by the most various sorts of ideologists. Whether it is, for example, a Bismark or a Bright (of the Anti-Corn Law League) that captures the anxieties of the bourgeois in an aristocratic society makes a great deal of difference in the resulting conception of the civic role of workers. For Bismark tries to isolate workers politically, Bright to recruit them in a political alliance against the aristocrats.

## IDENTIFICATION OF IDEOLOGICAL PROBLEMS

Bendix states a basic generalization that identifies ideological problems in the course of interpreting the meaning of a statement by Edmund Burke:

It is improbable of course that the early entrepreneurs were explicitly concerned with such problems or difficulties. Nevertheless, the fact that the ideological break with traditionalism was first undertaken on behalf of the ruling aristocracy *reveals the points of weakness at which ideological defenses were likely to be built*. There were two principal problems. How could the "higher classes" deny their responsibility for the poor and at the same time justify their power and authority over them? How could the poor be taught self-dependence without developing in them a dangerous independence? [WAI, p. 78; emphasis added].

The passage in italics gives Bendix's notion of the central internal dynamic of ideological development, that ideological elaboration takes place when received ideas justifying the social order conflict with the developing interests of the rulers. The traditional view justifying aristocratic authority in England was that authorities would take care of the poor, who could not take care of themselves. It was in the interests of entrepreneurs to deny that they had responsibilities beyond paying wages, and to assert that they should only pay wages when it would bring them profits. The "weaknesses" around which ideological defenses needed to be built were created by this contradiction between feudal justifications and bourgeois interests. In Russia, in contrast, the tsar was supposed to take care of the poor, not the aristocracy nor the bourgeoisie, who ideologically held their positions in society by appointment to the tsar, and ideas of self-dependence contradicted the overall authoritarian ideology of government.

The following quotations indicate some of the more general problems Bendix identifies as connected with industrial authority.

Industrialization in its early phase poses a very general problem. It is accompanied by the creation of a nonagricultural work force which is usually forced to bear the consequences of great social and economic dislocations. These dislocations terminate the traditional subordination of the 'lower classes' in the preindustrial society. Though this development varies considerably with the relative speed and with the social setting of industrialization, its result is that the 'lower classes' are deprived of their recognized, if subordinate, place in society. A major problem facing all societies undergoing industrialization is the civic integration of the newly created industrial work force [WAI, p. xxix].

All authority-relations have in common that those in command cannot fully control those who obey. To be effective, authority depends on the assumption that subordinates will follow instructions in terms of the spirit rather than the letter of the rules. Two things are implied here: that the subordinate will adopt the behavior alternatives selected for him, and that he will give his "good will" to carrying out his orders. As this formulation suggests, "good will" involves judgment and initiative. If these are withheld by a "withdrawal of efficiency" (Veblen), a slavish clinging to the letter of the rules, or active sabotage, then the subordinate uses his judgment for purposes of his own [*WAI*, p. xlv].

It should be noted, however, that their subordinates tend to acquire power even without authority to the extent that their expertise removes them from the effective control of their superiors. The tasks of management have increased in the sense that the increasing discretion of subordinates has had to be matched by strategies of organizational arrangements, material incentives, and ideological appeals if the ends of management were to be realized. In this respect the managerial ideologies of today are distinguished from the entrepreneurial ideologies of the past in that managerial ideologies are thought to aid employers or their agents in controlling and directing the activities of workers [*WAI*, p. 9].

Authority entails inescapable hazards not only because it is bound up with inequality, but because it must steer a course between being too forceful and not being forceful enough, between the arrogance of power and the failure of nerve [*WAI*, p. xlviii].

The ideas which are used to justify the exercise of authority in industry are employed primarily to justify the entrepreneurs before the public at large. That public consists typically of two major social groups, a politically dominant aristocracy and a newly recruited industrial force [*WAI*, p. 6].

In the West, the ideas which have been used to advance industrialization have reflected and affected the actions of entrepreneurs and managers of industry. These leaders of enterprise developed or made use of ideas which enhanced their social cohesion and active unity as a social class. Such cohesion and unity arise from the common interests of similarly situated individuals [*WAI*, p. 7].

Hence, the employer's authority as well as his earnings and privileges are the rewards of past and present exertions. For the people at large such rewards are promises held out for the future and little effort is made to disguise the heavy burden of labor. Most attempts to increase the present satisfactions of work consist rather in promises of future rewards and in benefits and appeals which have the character of additional incentives offered by the employer. Not one but all goals are offered to the individual as grounds for increasing his exertions: getting ahead and not falling behind, personal satisfaction and shining before others, more work and more leisure, individual accomplishment and teamwork, material possessions and spiritual values. The list of homilies is endless and all-embracing, and it is addressed to the masses of people who must find what comfort they can out of their single-handed efforts to reach these distant goals. In terms of ideology little is done to spare them their frustrations or to equivocate about the privilege and power of the few [*WAI*, p. 11].

What each of these general problems that produce "pressure to ideologize" have in common is that they point to historically important "weaknesses" in justificatory systems, points at which the interests of entrepreneurs (or in the case of p. 9, of modern managers with an intensified problem of "withdrawal of efficiency") come into conflict with the interests and ideas of people they depend on.

But the general guides about what sorts of problem to look for do not sufficiently describe the problems that an ideologist for a class has to deal with. An ideologist for entrepreneurs in Russia had to deal with the question of whether bourgeois ownership of serfs should be arranged on the same basis as rural landowners ownership of serfs, or whether, for example, rurally owned serfs should be forbidden to compete in their line of business. Obviously, no such problem occurred in England. Rather, the problem of the civic role of workers appeared in a context shaped by the specific features of the English poor law. In particular, the Speenhamland system, in which relief was given as a wage supplement to those whose wages were below subsistence levels, attacked the civic status of industrial workers.

And the idea of poor relief lost what little meaning had been left, since the rates were paid as a wage supplement, which was not their purpose, or the rate payment was evaded by confining the recipient in a workhouse and by exploiting his destitution. Henceforth workers were publicly stigmatized as paupers, whether they worked or not, since they were "on relief" in either case. It is not surprising that their self-respect vanished as the distinction between work and relief, between factory and workhouse, between diligence and indolence, disappeared. . . . Moreover, thoroughgoing reform could be accomplished only by combating the rapidly increasing demoralization of the working class. Yet to do so might increase the people's outrage, which was politically dangerous. Such measures would have presupposed that parliamentarians as well as leading groups of entrepreneurs had acquired an understanding of the workers' sense of degradation. The early industrialists, who were themselves engaged in a struggle for social recognition, proved to be incapable of such insight [WAI, p. 42-43].

Both the serf and the pauper present problems of the civic role of workers, and of how to pursue, for example, entrepeneurs' interests in labor mobility, in discipline and effort at work, in low wages, and in other aspects of authority in industry. But the institutional confusion of paupers and workers is a confusion different from the confusion of serfs and workers, embedded in different historical definitions of the moral nature and possibilities of personal development among the poor. The ideological problems of making pauperism and welfare less attractive than work are different from the Russian problems of justifying urban ownership of serfs.

## THE VARIETY OF IDEOLOGICAL PRODUCTS

There is an inherent dilemma in using ideological productions as evidence for a causal scheme like that of Bendix. On the one hand, unless people address the ideological problems that the analyst has identified, it is not clear that they are problems to the people. A general difficulty with "functional" arguments that explain social behavior as attempts to solve "system problems" of one sort or another is that people quite often solve the wrong problem, or give the wrong solution to the right problem.

Bendix is especially sensitive to this, for several reasons. First, one of his case studies, Russia, did not in fact "solve the problem" of justifying industrial authority, and had a proletarian revolution. Second, it is hard to imagine an ideologist providing a complex answer to a question he has failed to ask. Third, the identification of the historically shifting nature of problems people are addressing provides the basis of its own empirical criticism in a way that theories of universal functional problems do not. So ideological products have to be examined for evidence that they were really addressing identifiable problems of industrial authority.

On the other hand, a principal way to deal with ideological problems is to deny stridently that they exist. A main way for an ideologist to defend the interests of his own group is to ignore the problems his solution creates for others.

This dilemma is dealt with by Bendix in several ways. One is clearly to choose to analyze those ideological productions which satisfy the *two* criteria of having a relatively complete intellectual structure and yet being popular among entrepreneurs who do not usually think in book-length terms. Thus, the fact that Malthus explicitly addressed the dilemmas Bendix had identified in Burke's speech, by "showing" that poverty could not be relieved by generous upper classes, because generosity would cause increased population and greater poverty in the next generation, indicates that Bendix has correctly identified a dilemma felt by the people involved in the debate.

A second method, to me more convincing, is to show the variety of ideological productions with a common theme. More specifically, the common themes have to be the problems addressed, rather than the solutions proposed. If poverty is explained by character faults of the poor in evangelical writing that appeals to entrepreneurs, by hunger being a necessary motive to disciplined work by Townsend, by lack of reproductive restraint in Malthus, by being the state which entre- preneurs can rise out of by self-help (and hence implicitly a state of those who have not helped themselves) by Samuel Smiles, as a state caused by grasping landlords protected behind grain tariffs by John Bright, but is said to be caused by the greediness of capitalists only among aristocratic and labor ideologists, it indicates the recurrent problem of entrepreneurs and their ideologists to explain poverty in a way that does not under- mine their own authority or their honor in the political community (see *WAI*, pp. 64–73 for evangelicals, p. 74 for Townsend, pp. 78–86 for Malthus, pp. 109–115 for Smiles, and pp. 99–108 for Bright).


## ANALOGY BETWEEN INTELLECTUAL PRODUCTIONS

For the problems that Bendix addresses, then, the strategic links are those between general social developments and the dilemmas con- fronted by writers on social problems. Since Bendix is interested in the long-term effects of actions by legislators and managers and other people who read, he has to pay attention to literary products. What differentiates this from the work of literary critics or general historians of ideas, except perhaps the fact that Bendix requires that the literary products be popular in a given historical social group rather than per- manent achievements of Western civilization? What sort of discipline is his literary analysis subject to, that makes us think we are dealing with the fate of the civic role of workers rather than the maunderings of a second-rate demographer or a popularizer of early, crude free-trade economics?

Like the more social intellectual historians, Bendix traces themes through the writings of a group of men and women who respond to the same social conditions in a limited period of time. And as in these writings, the analogies of which the themes consist are constructed by a high ratio of historian's selectivity and historian's text to brief quotations of very unusual men. By the usual standards of "public opinion mea- surement" of entrepreneurial ideology, such a literary approach to highly selected people and texts might be excused because we cannot interview entrepreneurs of a century ago; but it is certainly not an ideal research procedure by modern standards. Is, then, the ring of truth in these accounts (a ring, incidentally, more convincing than public opin- ion polls in underdeveloped countries) merely a product of a gift for literary criticism, itself an art form rather than a science? No doubt it partly is: Coherence in history is partly a product of the coherence of books about history, and this is partly the product of the coherence of the overall theory of historical developments. But this is not all there is to it.

For example, consider this analogy between Malthus and Andrew Ure's, *The Philosophy of Manufactures*:

> In this defense of the manufacturers Ure did not make any reference to the Malthusian doctrine, and his references to population were confined to a survey of the labor force employed in the textile mills. Nevertheless, the two authors are related in the sense that Malthus' intellectual systematization and Ure's practical orientation toward the problems faced by the cotton manufacturers contained the same basic tenets. Both authors denied that the "higher classes" could take the responsibility of finding employment for the common people or of safeguarding them against extreme poverty and hunger. But where Malthus had demanded a generation earlier than the "higher classes" teach the people moral restraint as "the only effectual means of improving the condition of the poor," Ure maintained that the manufacturers were successfully meeting their obligations by the employment of men, women, and children [*WAI*, pp. 91–92].

The first point of analogy is in what the authors regard as inevitable, as outside the responsibility of entrepreneurs to remedy. An argument of inevitability is an argument of lack of responsibility. Although the causes beyond the ken of entrepreneurs are different (for Malthus, workers' reproductive habits; for Ure, workers exploiting their own children), the common location of the difficulty beyond the control of entrepreneurs diverts the blame. The second principle of blamelessness is closely related, that one is blameless if he "does the best he can," as evidenced either by humane concern with teaching workers to marry late or by giving employment on better terms than domestic industries. What is "the best he can" is obviously bound up with an analysis of what is possible, what is inevitable. But this in turn is bound up with an analysis of whether domestic industry, for example, can produce better wages and conditions: If it can, then better wages and conditions are obviously possible, and entrepreneurs are to blame.

The analogy thus consists of two sorts of judgments. The first has to do with the similarity of function of the two books, that they divert blame for miseries in the mills from entrepreneurs. The second is a similarity in deep intellectual structure, that blame is connected with ideas of causality (presumably this is a generalization about all humanity), and that there are various alternative causal ways to argue the same ideological point, that the entrepreneurs cannot do better.

Conversely, of course, there are various causal schemes that can argue the ideological point that workers can do better and hence that they are to blame for their poverty. For example, if workers did better, it would be in the entrepreneur's interest and within his capacity to reward them; they could live better if they did not spend their money on gin, if they had fewer children, if they had a philosophy of *Self Help*, and the like.

If all these are similar, then we can understand why Bendix urges that the agitation of the Anti-Corn Law League was a fundamental ideological break. For the basic point of this agitation was that workers could help solve the problem of poverty *by civic and political participation* in the reform movement. This implied both that workers could be trusted (better than aristocrats) with questions of public policy, and that the blame lay in political and legal arrangements, not in the vices of the poor.

# 4

# *Conclusion*

Now comes the time to assess where we have been. Our object has been to analyze how generality can be wrested from historical facts. The rhetorical structure of the book is made of a contrast between two psychologies of generality, two ideas about how the basic elements of theory are made.

Concepts are the things that capture aspects of the facts for a theory; they are the lexicon that the grammar of theory turns into general sentences about the world. The argument is that the power and fruitfulness of those sentences is determined by the realism and exactness of the lexicon of concepts, and not by the theoretical grammar. The problem of eliminating false sentences by research, the traditional problem of epistemology, is not as problematic as the problem of having sentences interesting enough to be worth accepting or rejecting. And this is determined by whether or not our concepts capture those aspects of reality that enter into powerful and fruitful causal sentences.

The agon that forms this rhetorical structure is between a psychology of generality that poses the dilemma between Kant and Nietzsche and one that urges that generality comes from research into the facts. That is, the argument is that the dilemma between synthetic reasoned generality, tested against the facts, and historical uniqueness, a portrait of the facts, is a false dilemma. The way out of the dilemma is that portraits of the facts, combined with an intellectual operation of carefully drawn analogies, are roads to generality.

There is nothing so likely to cause a misreading of this argument as twisting it back into the psychology of generality that it rejects. The Kantian versus Nietzsche (or positivist versus Dilthey) version of what epistemology is all about is so deeply embedded in the historical origins of social science that an argument based on the supposition that this is the wrong question has a hard time trying to say what it is about. The fact that the title of this book so strongly suggests a book different from the one I have written, that it suggests a book about Marxism and evolutionism and functionalism, is a symptom of the power of the epistemological psychology we have learned.

So first let me say what this book is not. First, it is not a book that says theory is no good to history. Second, it is not a book that denies that facts test theories, though it also suggests other intellectual functions for factual research. In short, it is not a book on the Nietzsche–Dilthey side of the argument. Its aim is Kantian, to say what it is about general ideas in historical research that makes them valuable and convincing. Third, it is also not an antiquantitative book, though I am doubtful about much of the quantitative history I have seen, and though none of the books analyzed were very quantitative. If the concept at the basis of the count is based on a deep causal analogy between the things counted, a number can be a most illuminating historical fact. Fourth, it is not a book about the epistemology of narrative, of linking together causal connections to explain a unique historical entity. All these views of what a book with this title might be are derived, I believe, from a false psychology of generality, that has been hooked on to a largely correct positivist epistemology.

What then does generality in concepts consist in? When we start research into a particular social change, we approach it with certain general notions: that the proletariat is important in revolutions, or that factory labor is distinctive in the way it separates work life from family life, or that every inegalitarian social order will produce among its rich an ideology about how the rich are not to blame for the poverty of the poor. This seems to confirm the epistemlogical psychology which says that general ideas come first, and the facts fit into them. The argument here is that such ideas are flaccid, that they are sufficient neither to guide historical research nor to give the resulting monograph the ring of having told us about the human condition. These ideas are good for introductions and conclusions, for 1-hour distinguished lectureships, for explaining briefly what our profession is all about, and for other functions in which easily comprehensible and inexact ideas are useful. They are not what good theory applied to historical information looks like, and consequently their being psychologically anterior has no epistemological significance. It is the fact that "theories of social change" consist of such flaccid general notions that makes them so much less interesting than studies of social changes. They are a gravy that helps flavor the meat, but the meat is in another sort of general ideas.

The meat of generality in historical studies of social change comes much nearer to the facts, in the body of the monograph. It does not generally come from prior notions, but from operations on the facts. The operation consists of drawing deep analogies between facts. What makes them deep analogies is their relation to the general causal argument at that point in the monograph. Let us now elaborate, with illustrative material from the monographs analyzed above, the definition we gave in Chapter 1 of a deep analogy.

## WHAT MAKES HUMAN ACTIONS ANALOGOUS?

The causal forces that make systematic social change go are people figuring out what to do. Instincts stay the same; functional prerequisites remain prerequisite; the cognitive content of people's minds changes. It changes in particular to take account of a new situation, so that cognitive change can have a cumulative and self-sustaining quality. What we have to study to understand history is how structural forces cause people to change their notions of what kind of situation they are in, and to sustain those new notions sufficiently long to build them into institutions that in turn sustain them.

Perhaps our purest case of this is Bendix, because he took as his fundamental problem explaining how the conception of the worker as a citizen could come about. It need not inevitably come about, as it did not in Tsarist Russia. The fundamental selective principle for the ideological materials analyzed in Bendix's monograph was that they should be the ideas about what workers were like that appealed to entrepreneurs and to their political representatives.

These ideas had to be appealing interpretations of the situation entrepreneurs found themselves in. These situations, in their turn, were different in Russia than in England, though there were some analogies that make it make sense to treat both in the same monograph. In both, the ideology that justified capitalist authority had to compete with an ideology of aristocratic landlords, but in one the rural workers were wage laborers working for large tenants, in the other a peasantry only lately and precariously out of serfdom. In both, entrepreneurs had to explain that urban poverty was not their fault, but in Russia the central government set wages and conditions of welfare payments, in England formally free labor individually accepted the wages offered and welfare payments were dispensed by local governments. In both countries, the question of who should represent worker interests in political society had to be answered, but in England it was a question of whether workers would vote for the capitalist party on the basis of free trade in grain; in Russia, workers did not vote for their representatives.

The central causal problem that interests Bendix in England is the origin of a conception of working men as participants in the polity, as capable of originating political objectives that ought to be respected in a well-run constitutional system. In particular, the slow, but real, consent of representatives of capitalist interests to a political role for workers needs explanation. For that reason, all ideological statements which do *not* link the solutions to problems of enterprise authority, poverty, the role of the aristocracy, to political responsibilities and rights of workers are roughly analogous. Those which do, from the electoral strategy of the Anti-Corn Law League to workers testifying to the factory inspectors, are likewise roughly analogous. The overall argument is that in England, but not in Russia, the entrepreneurial conception of the social system came to develop a component of a political and civic role for workers.

Whatever we think might have been the facts and importance of entrepreneurial consent to increasing political power of workers, the point here is clear: What Bendix is classifying (narratively) in one group or another are thoughts of men about what they ought to do.

But if we argue such a subjective view, are we not disintegrating structural and institutional concepts into erratic psychologism? What of macroscopic movements of history—it is not armies and modes of production that make history? Of course it is, and armies and modes of production have been in both chapters. To say that an army is men obeying does not make it (ordinarily—outside times of revolution) a random concatenation of whims. For the whole point is that people's definition of the situation they are in is powerfully determined by what situation they are in, and that is an institutional product. It was not the whim of the eighteenth-century French nobility that they should defend their privileges through *parlements* and turn over their public functions to an (noble) *Intendent*. Likewise, it was not a whim but a mode of production combined with technical changes that led hundreds of textile capitalists to make up their minds to decrease the ratio of spinners to helpers on the machines.

Thus the question is not whether we need structural concepts, but what we should build them out of. What an army consists of is a system for maintaining the definition of the situation, in each soldier's mind, that says he had better obey—the way armies break down in revolutions cannot be understood otherwise. What a mode of production consists of is what capitalists cannot help doing if they are to stay in business and make profits on their investments. What the public role of the nobility consists of is what they think they can do in *parlement* and what they think they can do in collecting the *taille* for use in local welfare over the opposition of the *Intendent*, who is obliged to send some of it to Paris. Thus these structural concepts—army, mode of production, nobility— have their causal force because they systematically shape people's cognitions.

The list of bedrock subjective concepts, out of which structural concepts are developed, usually consists of concepts of common-sense psychology: possibility (Can soldiers get away with it if they do not fire on the crowd?), constraint (How can a capitalist produce enough yarn?), reward (Will a capitalist make more profit with larger mules with many child-labor helpers?), effectiveness (Will the village land council let a peasant keep the land he just got?), causality (Did Russia lose to the Germans because of betrayals in the tsar's court?). Some are more subtle, but still talked about in common discourse, such as the question of Kerensky's tact (does he understand his place in the situation and what it requires?), or the question of alternative rhetorically effective ways to show that poverty was not the entrepreneurs' fault. Some may be deep social–psychological generalizations, such as perhaps the effect of military experience in politicizing Russian peasants. But institutions function, or fail to function, by affecting these elements of individual minds. An institution is a definition of the nature of reality for its participants. When it is not, it stops being an institution, and becomes perhaps a notion about social possibilities, a part of a reactionary utopia.

If all this is true, then our basic structural concepts have to be made up of components of what people want and what they think they have to do to get it. In Kenneth Burke's phrase, an institution or a mode of production is "a grammar of motive." Grand definitions that make us try to conceive the Tsarist army as, say, a realization of value commitments may or may not turn out to be crucial psychological observations, and hence structurally crucial. The only way to tell is to examine the acts that make up cohesion of that army, and to see how far they are similar in their value psychology, and differ from acts that constitute disintegration by differing value psychology. My impression is that Trotsky was right, that the Tsarist soldiers were scared not to obey.

But what this adds up to is that the concepts out of which our analysis of concrete social formation ought to be built up are made out of the materials got by analyzing the historical acts of which that social formation was in fact made up. Suppose that de Tocqueville is right that the legislative function of the English Parliament, and the local gentry structure of English local government, produced a different sort of nobility in England than was found in France—one whose privileges were legitimated by governmental functions. What this means is that, mode of production or not, the English nobility was a different social formation from the French nobility, particularly in its capacity to hold governmental power in the face of the growth of bourgeois economic power (actually also the mode of production in the strict sense in the richest parts of the English countryside was quite different from that in the richest parts of the French countryside). What made the nobility different was the different composition of acts that made up noble status. And what made *that* different was the different situation the English parliament, and the English country gentleman, thought they were in. One reason they thought differently about that situation was that the situation was in fact different.

Thus it is vain to seek sensible causal sentences about "nobilities" until we find out whether the nobilities were something like the same sort of thing in different countries. The only way to do that is to build up from analogies and differences among acts. And what makes acts causally analogous is similarity in what people want and what they think they need to do to get it.

The sort of theory we have been analyzing in the parts we have chosen from Bendix, Smelser, and the other analysts, comes in bits and pieces, rather than integrated systems of thought. This makes it hard to learn; to train oneself to be a "theorist" of social change one has to read a great many monographs by theoretically oriented social historians, store analogies and distinctions in one's mind, and hope that some of them give theoretical handles on new situations. But I believe that most of the examples analyzed in this book have some thematic unity in the materials of the basic concepts, though not a set of tight logical interconnections.

The first common feature is that some social structure is decomposed into problems confronting individuals in given social locations. The structure of the army creates problems for soldiers figuring out whether they will get shot for rebelling; the structure of spinning factories after 1820 creates problems for fathers in training and disciplining their children. Or more generally, a functional strain in a historical social system creates troubles for the people in it.

The direction that functional theory has gone when confronted with this problem is to try to locate analogies between functions in different systems. From de Tocqueville's attempt to locate the function of producing responsible statesmen by having vigorous autonomous local government to Bendix's generalization that all industrializing societies confront the problem of the civic role of the proletariat, the generalizing impulse among sociologists attaches itself most easily to the anatomy and physiology of social structures.

If the illustrations of this book are persuasive, they suggest that this is the wrong place to start on the long road to generality. For the causal forces in the situation are people defining problems and trying to work their way out of them. The functional strains or structural dilemmas in the system are, to be sure, the reasons why many people think they have the same problems. Idiosyncratic problems do not produce Russian or French revolutions, nor an entrepreneurial class in a political and ideological alliance with workers. But until a functional strain produces a common set of troubles for members of the system, its unity as a causal force is not established. Thus the elementary analogies, out of which wide ranging general concepts ought eventually to be constructed, are analogies between the thoughts of people about their situations, not analogies between structural dilemmas or functional strains of systems.

A second common feature of these examples is the utilitarian character of the explanations of individual actions. Trotsky's accounts of revolutionaries show sensible men calculating whether they can get what they want out of the Social Revolutionaries or out of the Bolsheviks, rather than Durkheimian revolutionary effervescence of a quasi-mystical kind. Certainly this is partly because I find such utilitarian theories more congenial, that utilitarian mechanisms sound to me more like the people I know, while ecstasy or commitment to ultimate values seem like weak and erratic causes. So I have selected historical analysts who have little touch with values and enthusiasms, or have selected parts of their work to analyze which are unrepresentative.

Given that caveat, I would argue that connections of social structures to the sensible plans of individuals are easier to construct than connections to their values and enthusiasms.

## THE LOGIC OF CONCEPTS

Now let us return to the epistemological point of the book in a more abstract form. The point is that an adjective or a noun, however completely defined, is not usually a very useful way to describe a scientific concept. It may make sense to define the number three as the set of all sets that have a count of three, but extending such a procedure to an empirical field tends to produce numerology rather than science. What we want of our classes is that their elements should play the same role in the structure of causal propositions, not that they should occur under the same entries in a dictionary. The problem of the epistemology of concept building is to maximize the similarity of the causal role of things classified together, and their difference from things classified elsewhere.

There are roughly two strategies for doing this, one of which concentrates on the truth of the general sentences, and one of which looks for similar elementary sentences. Using the first one, we take a general sentence, such as, "Nobilities tend to be overthrown with the growth of capitalism." We find contrary cases, many noblemen in the English Parliament at the beginning of the twentieth century, a nobility killed off en masse by a Russian tsar, feudalism abolished by a land reform of a Serbian king. Then we try to find enough differentiating adjectives for "nobility" in the first part of the proposition so that it becomes true, or enough alternative agencies of overthrow besides capitalism in the second part to include tsars and Serbian kings.

The alternative strategy is to look for more elementary sentences involving a causal connection, such as, "A lot of soldiers in Petersburg did not think they would be shot for rebelling, and so were easier to recruit; I wonder who exactly was scared, and who was not, in the army as a whole." Then, insofar as we find a great many instances of people who conceive of the possibility of rebelling in some social locations, and a great many who do not in others, we build up a concept of disciplined and undisciplined situations. Because of the way we have built it, the invention of the concept and the assertion of the causal generalization are more or less the same acts. The theory is built as a carpenter builds, adjusting the measurements as he goes along, rather than as an architect builds, drawing first, building later.

The argument of this book is that most generality obtained in the first way, by adding enough particulars to make the generalization true, is specious generality. At any time it claims the unproven cases. Mostly when the cases come in, they require further particularizations.

The difficulty with the strategy advocated here is that a particular causal judgment in historical work has no chance of being wrong. The sentence, "Soldier X was not afraid and he did not shoot the workers," is either factually true or not. "Soldier X was not afraid, so he did not shoot the workers," was the sort of sentence Hume worried about.

Consequently, the epistemological argument rests on being able to make pretty good guesses about the place of particular acts in the causal scheme. When we show that mules produced yarn a lot cheaper than hand spinning in India, but handloom weavers could compete with mechanical looms, and we know something about capitalist organization in Manchester, we are not surprised that a lot of spinning factories and only a few weaving factories grew up. The place in the causal scheme of the act of installing mules, and not installing automatic looms, in a particular factory is pretty obvious. This need not be the case, and the scientist's general suspicion of historical "interpretation" is justified.

The same problem, however, plagues the improvement of a causal generalization with limiting modifiers. I have suggested, for example, that de Tocqueville reached desperately for nondistinguishing distinctions to explain why the English nobility was not overthrown. That is, knowing the English nobility was not overthrown, de Tocqueville searched for sufficient adjectives distinguishing that nobility from the French nobility so that he could blame the Revolution on inadequacies of the nobility. But this is equally precarious post hoc "interpretation" as the judgment of a particular act. The reason the same problem applies in both places is that the strategies are logically equivalent. Their difference is psychological.

For both strategies, a causal generalization can be disproved only after it has been stated in general form. For both, once it has been disproved one has to look at the facts for the contrary cases in order to reach for generality again. Why then make a big wind about the difference between two equivalent procedures? The reason is that the usual account of the "synthetic reason" procedure is usually truncated when the scientist knows his or her generalization is false, and does not say much about how to get another, truer, one.

Since a class is logically the same thing as a set of equivalences among members of a class, a causal generalization in historical materials is a set of analogies between particular causal assertions. A causal generalization is, "When royal governments have outlived their usefulness, weak kings or tsars reign without governing and fall easily." This is equivalent to asserting an analogy between the statement, "Tsar Alexander's unwillingness or inability to decide what to do about the war caused events that led to revolution," and "Louis XVI's lack of clarity about the purposes and role of the Estates General caused events that led to revolution." When the generalization appears in a history of the Russian Revolution, it appears as an "interpretation," and has no particular claim to generality. By the simple act of asserting that two instances are alike, however, a class, a concept, is created, a generalization about it is offered, some evidence is brought forth, and we are embarked on a scientific enterprise. A detailed analysis of what the tsar wanted from his cabinet and the Duma, what Louis XVI wanted from the Estates General, and in what respects these were similar, sets us on the path of giving a realistic and useful definition of the waffle-word "weak" in the generalization.

The moral of this book is that great theorists descend to the level of such detailed analogies in the course of their work. Further, they become greater theorists down there among the details, for it is the details that theories in history have to grasp if they are to be any good.

# References

Bendix, Reinhard
  1956  *Work and authority in industry.* New York: Wiley.
de Jouvenel, Bertrand
  1947  *On power,* translated by J. F. Huntington. New York: Viking, Translation published 1949.
de Tocqueville, Alexis
  1856  *The Old Regime and the French revolution,* translated by Stuart Gilbert. Garden City: Doubleday Anchor. Translation published 1955.
Duncan, Beverley, and Stanley Lieberson
  1970  *Metropolis and region in transition.* Beverley Hills: Sage Publications.
Goffman, Erving
  1963  *Behavior in public places.* New York: Free Press.
Marx, Karl
  1851  *The 18th Brumaire of Louis Bonaparte.* New York: International Publishers. Translated from a German version, reprinted 1935.
Marx, Karl and Frederick Engels
  1888  *Manifesto of the Communist party.* London: Reeves.
Nietzsche, Friedrich Wilhelm
  1887  *Zur Geneologie der Moral.* In *Werke,* Volume 2, edited by Karl Schlechter, Munich: Karl Hanser. Reprinted 1966.

Parsons, Talcott
  1966  *Societies: Evolutionary and comparative perspectives*. Englewood Cliffs, N.J.: Prentice-Hall.
  1971  *The system of modern societies*. Englewood Cliffs, N.J.: Prentice-Hall.
Smelser, Neil J.
  1959  *Social change in the industrial revolution*. Chicago: University of Chicago Press; London: Routledge and Kegan Paul.
  1962  *Theory of collective behavior*. New York: Free Press.
Stinchcombe, Arthur L.
  1974  *Creating efficient industrial administrations*. New York: Academic Press.
Stretton, Hugh
  1969  *The political sciences*. New York: Basic Books.
Trotsky, Leon
  1932  *History of the Russian Revolution*, translated by Max Eastman. New York: Simon and Schuster. Translated 1932 more or less simultaneously with the Russian version. Reprinted in 1 volume with the original 3-volume pagination by University of Michigan Press, 1960.
Weber, Max
  1904–1905  *The Protestant ethic and the spirit of capitalism*, translated by Talcott Parsons. London: G. Allen Unwin. Translation published 1930.
  1921–1922  *The theory of social and economic organization*, translated by A. M. Henderson and Talcott Parsons. New York: Oxford University Press. Translation published 1947.

# Index

Numbers in italics refer to the pages on which the complete references are listed.

**A**

Abstraction, 73–74
Adjectives, attached to power to make authority, 51
AGIL, 80–81
Analogy, 17–22
  deep, 21, 29
Anarchism, 58–59
Anti-Corn Law League, see Bright, John
Apprenticeship, 92–93
  not viable in power loom factories, 98–99
Army, 35, 39, 46, 57, 64, 118–119, 122
  and proletariat contrasted, 52–53
Attributes produced by relations, 32
Authority, 33–51, 106–108
  authoritative purposes, 37–41

**B**

Bankruptcy, of a social regime, 33–34
Bedazzlements, 25
Bendix, Reinhard, 23, 104–113, 117–118, *125*
Bolsheviks, 19–20, 51–55
Bolton spinner, 86, 95
Bonapartism, 13
Bright, John, 111
Bureaucracy, see Royal bureaucracy

Burke, Edmund, 106–107, 110–112
Burke, Kenneth, 119

**C**

Calvinism, 70–71, 73–75
Canada, 55–56
Capital city, 49
Capitalism, 8–9, 65–66, 74
Causal fruitfulness, 28
Causal statements, 17–22, 25–29
Censorship, 56, 58
Child labor, 92–93
  by occupation of father and widowhood of mother, 100
  not hired by family in weaving factories, 98–99
Children, 84, 87–97, see also Apprenticeship, Child labor, Wild children
Civil servants, 37
Classes, see Logic
Collective behavior, technical discussion of, 83–87
Combined and uneven development, 65–68
Competence, 36, 39, 59–61, 64–65
Compromisers, see Social Revolutionary party
Conflict, intensification of, 65–68

Cooperative
  communities, 85, 96
  stores, 85–86
Corporately organized groups, 25–29
Cumulative causation, 61–70

**D**
Defeats, 38
de Jouvenel, Bertrand, 8, *125*
Democracy, 38, 41–42
Deprivation, 33–34
de Tocqueville, Alexis, 11, 19, 31–75,
  *125*
Dickens, Charles, 36
Differential equations, 66–69
Differentiation, *see* Social differentia-
  tion
Dispositions, *see* Predispositions of
  systems
Distinctions
  effortful social, 44
Disturbance, 83–87
Dual power, 35–36, 40–41, 46, 49–50
Duma, 37
Duncan, Beverley, 8, *125*

**E**
Education, 84
Effectiveness, 34, 40
Efficiency, 15–16, 36, *see also* Effective-
  ness
Engels, Frederick, *125*
England, compared with France, 44
Epochal interpretations, 7–13
Equivalence relations, 21, *see also*
  Analogy
Estates General, 37, 39, 123
Executive organs, 14–16
Experience of public affairs, *see* Com-
  petence

**F**
Families, in spinning, 87–97
Feudalism, 8–9, 34, 50, 65–66
Field of choice, *see* Virtual choice ideal
  types

Functional explanation, 81–83, 89–91,
  99–102, 110–111, 120, 121, *see also*
  Social differentiation

**G**
Geertz, Clifford, 25 n
Generality, 2–3, 22, *see also* Analogy,
  Kant, Positivism
Geographical distribution, 51–56
Goffman, Erving, 27, *125*
Good will, 107

**H**
Hobsbawm, E. J., 25 n
Hours, 95–97, 100–102

**I**
Ideal sequence, 89–97, *see also* Narra-
  tive
Ideal types, 61–75
Ideas
  and possibilities, 34
  new irresponsible, 102–104
Ideology, 104–113, *see also* Symbols
Incapacity, 36, *see also* Competence
Incompetence, *see* Competence
Industrialization, 107
Inequality, 42–46, 108
Inevitability, 37–41, *see also* Uncer-
  tainty
Institutionalization, 60–61
Integrity, 97
Intellectuals, 39–40, 56, 69
Intelligence as a special kind of pre-
  disposition, 59–61

**J**
Jenny, *see* Machinery in cotton manufacture

**K**
Kadets, 12, 19–20
Kant, Immanuel, 3, 115–117
Kerensky, Aleksandr, 72–74

**L**
Land committees, 38
Langedoc, 55
Law, 71–72
Learning, rates of, 68
Legitimacy, 15–16
Lenin, Vladimir, 14–16, 51–55
Liberalism, 58–59
Liberty, 41–42
Lieberson, Stanley, 8, *125*
Logic, 17–22, 25–29, 121–124
Logical positivism, *see* Positivism
Louis XVI, 123

**M**
Machinery in cotton manufacture, 84,
 91–95, 97–99, 123
Malthus, Thomas, 110–112
Marx, Karl, 7–13, 76, *125*
Mode of production, 118–120
Modernism, 10
Molecular processes, 38, 52
Monarchy, 31–32
Mule, *see* Machinery in cotton manu-
 facture

**N**
Names of concepts, 10–12, 24–25
Narrative
 as a literary device, 11–12
 theoretical character of, 13–16
Nationalities, 36, 51–55
Nietzsche, Friedrich, 16, 115–117, *125*
Nobility, 33, 34, 43–47, 118–119, 122

**O**
Oastler, 85

**P**
Parsons, Talcott, 7–13, 80–81, *126*
Parties, political, 51–55
Peasants, 35–36, 38, 43, 48
Peterloo, 99
Petersburg, 51–55
Petty bourgeois party, 10
Political parties, *see* Parties

Poor law, 109
Positivism, 3–7, 24, 27, 115–117
Possibilities, 34, 47–48, 53–55
Power loom, *see* Machinery in cotton
 manufacture, Weavers
Power of government, 8–9
Predicate, *see* Attributes produced
 by relations, Logic
Prediction, 27
Predispositions of systems, 56–61
Property rights, 39, 59, *see also* Attri-
 butes produced by relations
Putting out system, 89–91

**Q**
Quakers, 70–71, 73–75
Quantitative methods, 4–7, 53–54,
 66–69

**R**
Rates of change, 68–69
Reduced form of equations, 9
Relations produce attributes, 32
Relative deprivation, *see* Deprivation
Religion, 48
Representative organs, 14–16
Responsibility for the poor, 107–113
Revolution, 33–75
 as contrasted with normal politics,
 66–68
Roman law, 71–72
Royal bureaucracy, 36–37, 50, 55, 59,
 69

**S**
St. Petersburg, *see* Petersburg
Savings banks, 82, 86–87
Sects, Protestant, 70–71, 73–75, 100
Self-dependence, 107
Sequence, *see,* Ideal sequence, Narra-
 tive
Smelser, Neil J., 23, 77–104, *126*
Smiles, Samuel, 111
Social differentiation, 77–81
Social field, 61, *see also* Social order
Social order, 28, *see also* Social field

Social Revolutionary party, 19–20, 24, 35, 51–55, 62–64
Speenhamland system, 109
Spinning jenny, see Machinery in cotton manufacture
Spontaneity, 33
Stalin, Joseph, 13–16
Stalinism, 14–16
Stratification, governmental in de Tocqueville, 42–43
Stretton, Hugh, 22, 126
Strikes, 94, 97
Symbols, 48–49, see also Ideology of deference, 45
Synthetic reason, 3

T
Tact, 72–74, 119
Taxation, 43–44
Ten hours bill, 95–97
Tilly, Charles, 25 n
Tithes, 34
Trade unions, 92–93
Trotsky, Leon, 11, 14–16, 19, 31–75, 126
Tsar Alexander, 123
Tseretelli, 36

U
Uncertainty, 35, 37–41, 56–61
Ure, Andrew, 112
Utopianism, 96

V
Value added reasoning, 79–80
Values, 78–79, 97
Vanguard, 49
Veblen, Thorstein, 108
Venality of office, 36
Verifiability, see Positivism
Virtual choice ideal types, 62–63, 70–75
Voting statistics, 54
Vyborg district of Petersburg, 51–55

W
Wage levels, 94–95
Water frame, see Machinery in cotton manufacture
Weavers, 85, 97–99
Weber, Max, 22, 70–71, 73–75, 100, 126
Wild children, 84 ,87, 95
World system, 65–68

# STUDIES IN SOCIAL DISCONTINUITY

*Under the Consulting Editorship of:*

CHARLES TILLY
*University of Michigan*

EDWARD SHORTER
*University of Toronto*

*William A. Christian, Jr.* Person and God in a Spanish Valley

*Joel Samaha.* Law and Order in Historical Perspective: The Case of Elizabethan Essex

*John W. Cole and Eric R. Wolf.* The Hidden Frontier: Ecology and Ethnicity in an Alpine Valley

*Immanuel Wallerstein.* The Modern World-System: Capitalist Agriculture and the Origins of the European World-Economy in the Sixteenth Century

*John R. Gillis.* Youth and History: Tradition and Change in European Age Relations 1770 – Present

*D. E. H. Russell.* Rebellion, Revolution, and Armed Force: A Comparative Study of Fifteen Countries with Special Emphasis on Cuba and South Africa

*Kristian Hvidt.* Flight to America: The Social Background of 300,000 Danish Emigrants

*James Lang.* Conquest and Commerce: Spain and England in the Americas

*Stanley H. Brandes.* Migration, Kinship, and Community: Tradition and Transition in a Spanish Village

*Daniel Chirot.* Social Change in a Peripheral Society: The Creation of a Balkan Colony

*Jane Schneider and Peter Schneider.* Culture and Political Economy in Western Sicily

*Michael Schwartz.* Radical Protest and Social Structure: The Southern Farmers' Alliance and Cotton Tenancy, 1880-1890

*Ronald Demos Lee* (Ed.). Population Patterns in the Past

*David Levine.* Family Formations in an Age of Nascent Capitalism

*Dirk Hoerder.* Crowd Action in Revolutionary Massachusetts, 1765-1780

*Charles P. Cell.* Revolution at Work: Mobilization Campaigns in China

*Frederic L. Pryor.* The Origins of the Economy: A Comparative Study of Distribution in Primitive and Peasant Economies

*Harry W. Pearson.* The Livelihood of Man by Karl Polanyi

*Richard Maxwell Brown and Don E. Fehrenbacher* (Eds.). Tradition, Conflict, and Modernization: Perspectives on the American Revolution

*Juan G. Espinosa and Andrew S. Zimbalist.* Economic Democracy: Workers' Participation in Chilean Industry 1970-1973

*Arthur L. Stinchcombe.* Theoretical Methods in Social History

*In preparation*

*Randolph Trumbach.* The Rise of the Egalitarian Family: Aristocratic Kinship and Domestic Relations in Eighteenth-Century England

*H. A. Gemery and J. S. Hogendorn* (Eds.). The Uncommon Market: Essays in the Economic History of the Atlantic Slave Trade

*Tamara K. Hareven* (Ed.). Transitions: The Family and the Life Course in Historical Perspective